ART THERAPY

DATE DUE

CREATIVE THERAPIES IN PRACTICE

The *Creative Therapies in Practice* series, edited by Paul Wilkins, introduces and explores a range of arts therapies, providing trainees and practitioners alike with a comprehensive overview of theory and practice. Drawing on case material to demonstrate the methods and techniques involved, the books are lively and informative introductions to using the creative arts in therapeutic practice.

Books in the series:

Psychodrama
Paul Wilkins

Dance Movement Therapy
Bonnie Meekums

Music Therapy
Rachel Darnley-Smith and Helen M. Patey

PRAISE FOR ART THERAPY

'I believe that David Edwards' book is an excellent introduction for all of those wishing to increase their knowledge concerning the profession of art therapy. Readers will particularly appreciate David's ability to clearly convey complex material which includes psychotherapeutic concepts, illustrated case histories, and historical to the present day developments within the profession. A readable and accessible overview which will contribute to a greater understanding of the profession of art therapy and the therapeutic use of art undertaken by registered art therapists.'

Carole Pembrooke
Chair of the British Association of Art Therapists

'Vivid clinical vignettes and remarkable illustrations combine to give a lively sense of art therapy in action. They bring the reader right into the art therapy studio. David Edwards locates the practice of art therapy firmly in its historical and cultural context, explaining its roots in art and links to psychoanalysis, in this always engaging account. The detailed bibliography and resources section offers a foundation for further exploration as well as information about training. An excellent introduction to the topic, this book will be invaluable for beginners, students and experienced practitioners alike.'

Professor Joy Schaverien
Jungian Analyst in private practice and Visiting Professor in Art
Psychotherapy at the University of Sheffield

ART THERAPY

David Edwards

⑤SAGE Publications
London • Thousand Oaks • New Delhi

SAGE Publications Ltd
1 Oliver's Yard
55 City Road
London EC1Y 1SP

SAGE Publications Inc.
2455 Teller Road
Thousand Oaks, California 91320

SAGE Publications India Pvt Ltd
B-42, Panchsheel Enclave
Post Box 4109
New Delhi 110 017

British Library Cataloguing in Publication data

A catalogue record for this book is available
from the British Library

ISBN 0 7619 4750 7
ISBN 0 7619 4751 5 (pbk)

Library of Congress Control Number available

Typeset by C&M Digitals (P) Ltd., Chennai, India
Printed and bound in Great Britain by Athenaeum Press, Gateshead

CONTENTS

LIST OF FIGURES

PREFACE

A rt therapy, or art psychotherapy as it is increasingly referred to, has changed considerably since I entered the profession in 1982. At that time most art therapists worked in the large asylums located on the fringes of our major cities and art therapy training was in its relative infancy. Furthermore, art therapy had yet to become a fully recognised NHS profession in the UK, there were no published codes of ethics to guide art therapists in their work, access to appropriate clinical supervision was often problematic, while continuing professional development and evidence based practice had yet to exert the influence they now do. In the early 1980s the published literature on the subject was also sparse, with what books there were on art therapy being primarily North American in origin and often difficult to obtain. Indeed, it was not until 1984 that the first book to provide a contemporary perspective on art therapy in the UK was published (Dalley, 1984).

Over the past two decades, as the asylums closed and new employment opportunities emerged, art therapists have extended their work into new areas and the available literature on art therapy has substantially increased. Books on art therapy appear with increasing frequency, although much of this literature is written for the specialist rather than the general reader. In common with the other books in the 'Creative Therapies in Practice' series, this book aims to provide a clearly written, accessible and informative introduction to art therapy in a style that does not assume prior knowledge of the discipline. While I hope it will be of relevance to practicing art therapists in the UK and elsewhere, this book has been written primarily for students, therapists and academics in related disciplines, prospective clients and anyone who may be interested in exploring the potential of art therapy to promote their own personal growth.

Chapter 1 addresses the deceptively simple question 'What is art therapy?' In this chapter I describe what art therapy is, and what it is not, in addition to outlining what it uniquely has to offer, where it is practiced and with whom. Chapters 2 and 3 are concerned with the history and development of the profession. The first of these chapters traces the origins of those ideas that have shaped the development of art therapy, including developments in the visual arts, psychiatry and psychoanalysis. Chapter 3 is more specifically concerned with the development of the art therapy profession in the UK. Chapter 4 explores the theoretical basis of art therapy, paying particular attention to the ways in which theories derived from psychoanalysis have been employed in order to help art therapists better understand the therapeutic process and the images clients make. Chapter 5 examines a range of issues concerned with the clinical practice of art therapy; including assessment, individual and group art therapy, using themes and endings. In Chapter 6 I discuss the training art therapists receive in the UK. My exploration of this topic involves an examination of the way art therapy trainings are organised, along with questions concerning who trains to be an art therapist and why? Chapter 7 discusses the professional infrastructure supporting the practice of art therapy in the UK. Particular attention is paid to the registration of art therapists, codes of ethics and professional practice, supervision, continuing professional development and research. Because art therapy has emerged in different contexts, the final chapter, Chapter 8, offers an international perspective on art therapy. This chapter outlines the development of the art therapy profession in Europe, the USA, Canada and Australia. Throughout the book images and case material are used to illustrate the process of art therapy. These are in italic type. To protect confidentiality, the names of clients have been changed and details of the cases described altered or disguised.

In choosing to write about art therapy from such a wide perspective, I am acutely aware of the limitations of this book. Due to the nature of my own work, which has been primarily in adult mental health, the case material discussed does not include work with children, the elderly or clients with learning and other disabilities. Moreover, given the book's scope, it has not always been possible to pay my subject the detailed attention it merits. I have, therefore, provided two appendices intended to help the reader fill in for themselves any perceptible gaps in my text. The first of these appendices is an introductory reading list. In addition to referencing the majority of important recent contributions to the art therapy literature, particularly in the UK, this reading list also covers many of the specialist areas in which art therapists now work. Appendix 2 provides up-to-date sources of largely internet based information on art therapy and related subjects, including professional organizations and training.

David Edwards, Sheffield

ACKNOWLEDGEMENTS

There are many people I should like to thank for their contribution to the writing of this book. Firstly, I wish to thank the many clients I have worked with over the years. This book is dedicated to them. Secondly, I wish to express my gratitude to the staff and students at Goldsmiths College, University of London, and to my former colleagues at Brookside Young Peoples Unit in Ilford, Essex (circa 1980–82). It was during this time that I began to acquire the skills necessary to practice and survive as an art therapist. Particular thanks are due here to Dr Andrea Gilroy, Professor Renos Papadopoulos, Dr K.S. Perinpanyagam and to Terry and Sarah Molloy.

I would like also to thank the many staff and students I have worked with on the art therapy training courses run by the University of Sheffield, especially Clare Hughes, David Maclagan, Professor Joy Schaverien and Dr Chris Wood. Many of the ideas and issues explored in this book first began to take shape through my involvement in the training of art therapists and I am grateful to have had this opportunity.

Thanks are also due to the past and present editors of *Inscape*, the Journal of the British Association of Art Therapists, for their support over many years. I am particularly indebted to Helen Greenwood and Sally Skaife, both of whom have encouraged me to write more clearly, use shorter sentences and fewer footnotes than I would otherwise be inclined to do.

I would like to express my appreciation to those individuals who have been more immediately involved in the writing of this book. To Ainslie Green who read and provided helpful comments on early drafts of the book, and to Professor Diane Waller, Joan Phillips (ATR-BC), Eva-Marie Stern, Jacqueline Fehlner, John Henzell, Jill Westwood and Annette Coulter who kindly supplied me with additional background material on art therapy in Europe, the USA, Canada and Australia. I should also like to thank my editor, Paul Wilkins, for his help in shaping this book and the editorial and production staff at Sage for their patience and understanding.

Finally, I should like to thank my parents, George and Betty Edwards, my partner Julie Leeson and my children, Carmen and Oliver. Without their love and support my life would have been very different and this book would never have been written.

1

WHAT IS ART THERAPY?

Numerous and often conflicting definitions of art therapy have been advanced since the term, and later the profession, first emerged in the late 1940s (Waller and Gilroy, 1978). In the UK, the artist Adrian Hill is generally acknowledged to have been the first person to use the term 'art therapy' to describe the therapeutic application of image making. For Hill, who had discovered the therapeutic benefits of drawing and painting while recovering from tuberculosis, the value of art therapy lay in 'completely engrossing the mind (as well as the fingers) … [and in] releasing the creative energy of the frequently inhibited patient' (Hill, 1948: 101–102). This, Hill suggested, enabled the patient to 'build up a strong defence against his misfortunes' (Hill, 1948: 103).

At around the same time, Margaret Naumberg, a psychologist, also began to use the term art therapy to describe her work in the USA. Naumberg's model of art therapy based its methods on,

> Releasing the unconscious by means of spontaneous art expression; it has its roots in the transference relation between patient and therapist and on the encouragement of free association. It is closely allied to psychoanalytic theory … Treatment depends on the development of the transference relation and on a continuous effort to obtain the patient's own interpretation of his symbolic designs … The images produced are a form of communication between patient and therapist; they constitute symbolic speech. (Naumberg in Ulman, 2001: 17)

Although the approaches to art therapy adopted by Hill and Naumberg were very different, and have been superseded by subsequent developments within the profession, their pioneering work has nevertheless exercised a significant influence. Essentially, Naumberg's position might be described as championing the use of art *in* therapy, whereas Hill advocated art *as* therapy. Subtle though this distinction may at first appear, it is of crucial importance in understanding art therapy as it is practiced today. This is because art therapy has developed along 'two parallel strands: art as therapy and art psychotherapy' (Waller, 1993: 8). The first of these approaches emphasises the healing potential of art, whereas the second

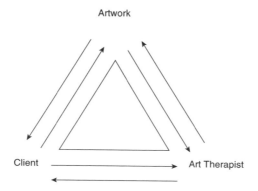

Artwork

Client ⟶ Art Therapist

1.1 *Triangular relationship*

stresses the importance of the therapeutic relationship established between the art therapist, the client and the artwork. The importance accorded to these respective positions is central to the whole question of where healing or therapeutic change in art therapy takes place. That is to say, whether this is due primarily to the creative process itself, to the nature of the relationship established between client and therapist or, as many art therapists would now argue, to a synthesis of the varied and subtle interactions between the two (Schaverien, 1994; Skaife, 1995). In art therapy this dynamic is often referred to as the triangular relationship (Case, 1990, 2000; Schaverien, 1990, 2000; Wood, 1990).

Within this triangular relationship greater or lesser emphasis may be placed on each axis (between, for example, the client and their art work or between the client and the art therapist) during a single session or over time.

Towards a Definition of Art Therapy

As the profession of art therapy has established itself, definitions have become more settled. From a contemporary perspective, art therapy may be defined as a form of therapy in which creating images and objects plays a central role in the psychotherapeutic relationship established between the art therapist and client. The British Association of Art Therapists, for example, defines art therapy in the following terms,

> Art therapy is the use of art materials for self-expression and reflection in the presence of a trained art therapist. Clients who are referred to an art therapist need not have previous experience or skill in art, the art therapist is not primarily concerned with making an aesthetic or diagnostic assessment of the client's image. The overall aim of its practitioners is to enable a client to effect change

and growth on a personal level through the use of art materials in a safe and facilitating environment. (BAAT, 2003)

Other national professional associations provide similar, but subtly different, definitions. The American Art Therapy Association defines art therapy as:

The therapeutic use of art making, within a professional relationship, by people who experience illness, trauma, or challenges in living, and by people who seek personal development. Through creating art and reflecting on the art products and processes, people can increase awareness of self and others, cope with symptoms, stress, and traumatic experiences; enhance cognitive abilities; and enjoy the life-affirming pleasures of making art. (from the AATA website, 2003)

In a similar vein, the Canadian Art Therapy Association and the Australian National Art Therapy Association define art therapy in the following terms,

Art therapy is a form of psychotherapy that allows for emotional expression and healing through nonverbal means. Children, unlike most adults, often cannot easily express themselves verbally. Adults, on the other hand may use words to intellectualise and distance themselves from their emotions. Art therapy enables the client to break through these cumbersome barriers to self-expression using simple art materials. (from the CATA website, 2003)

[Art therapy is] a form of psychotherapy, [that] is an interdisciplinary practice across health and medicine, using various visual art forms such as drawing, painting, sculpture and collage … Generally, it is based on psychoanalytic or psychodynamic principles, but all therapists are free to utilise whatever theoretical base they feel comfortable with. (from the ANATA website, 2003)

The essence of art therapy lies in the relationship it is possible to establish between art and therapy. That this relationship between the two disciplines might contain the potential for conflict, as well as healing, has resulted in its being described as an 'uneasy partnership' (Champernowne, 1971). As M. Edwards comments,

It seems that sometimes one or other partner gives up the struggle so that we have art without much therapy or therapy without much art. In either case the specific advantage of the relationship between these two disciplines is lost. (1981: 18)

It is important to note here that in art therapy this relationship is specifically focused on the visual arts (primarily painting, drawing and sculpting) and does not usually include the use of other art forms like music, drama or dance. While there may be some overlap between these different disciplines (see Hamer, 1993; Jennings and Minde, 1995), in the UK the therapeutic application of these arts is undertaken by therapists who, like art therapists, have received a specialised training (Darnley-Smith and Patey, 2003; Meekums, 2002; Wilkins, 1999). This is not, however, the situation elsewhere in Europe. As Waller (1999: 47–48), observes, in the Netherlands 'these professions are known as creative therapy and are much more closely linked in terms of training and professional development' (see Chapter 8).

The Aims of Art Therapy

In practice, art therapy involves both the process and products of image making (from crude scribbling through to more sophisticated forms of symbolic expression) *and* the provision of a therapeutic relationship. It is within the supportive environment fostered by the therapist–client relationship that it becomes possible for individuals to create images and objects with the explicit aim of exploring and sharing the meaning these may have for them. It is by these means that the client may gain a better understanding of themselves and the nature of their difficulties or distress. This, in turn, may lead to positive and enduring change in the client's sense of self, their current relationships and in the overall quality of their lives. As Storr (1972: 203) observes, creativity offers a means of 'coming to terms with, or finding symbolic solutions for, the internal tensions and dissociations from which all human beings suffer in varying degree'.

The aims of art therapy often vary according to the particular needs of the individuals with whom the art therapist works. These needs may change as the therapeutic relationship develops. For one person the process of art therapy might involve the art therapist encouraging them to share and explore an emotional difficulty through the creation of images and discussion; whereas for another it may be directed towards enabling them to hold a crayon and make a mark, thereby developing new ways of giving form to previously unexpressed feelings. While it is often assumed to be so, it is not the case that only those individuals who are technically proficient in the visual arts are able to make use of art therapy in a beneficial way. Indeed an emphasis on artistic ability – as might be the case when art is used primarily for recreational or educational purposes – is likely to obscure that with which art therapy is most concerned. That is to say, with the symbolic expression of feeling and human experience through the medium of art.

What Art Therapy Is, and What It Is Not

Although art therapy has developed considerably from its informal and ill-defined beginnings, an unfortunate legacy of myth and misunderstanding concerning its aims and methods still remains. As a consequence, the term 'art therapy' continues to be applied uncritically to a wide variety of therapeutic art activities (Richardson, 2001). All too frequently art therapy is viewed as a skill or technique, rather than a distinct therapeutic modality. Perhaps the most obvious reason for this is that members of other professional groups have used art or image making for recreational, diagnostic or therapeutic purposes. These professions include community and hospital based artists (Kaye and Blee, 1997; Senior and Croall, 1993), psychiatrists (Birtchnell, 1986; Cunningham Dax, 1998; Meares, 1958; Pickford, 1967), occupational therapists (Henare et al., 2003; Lloyd and Papas, 1999), nurses (Bentley, 1989; Clarke and Willmuth, 1982; Jones, 2000) and social workers (Braithwaite, 1986) among others. As the members of each of these diverse groups bring with them a particular approach to the image, the work of art therapists may occasionally be obscured in the resulting confusion concerning who does what. This can, regrettably, lead to boundary disputes between different disciplines and misunderstanding in the minds of colleagues and potential clients.

Art Therapy and Occupational Therapy

One profession with which art therapy has often been mistaken with respect to the therapeutic application of art is occupational therapy. There appear to be two main reasons for this. Firstly, the respective histories of art therapy and occupational therapy are inextricably linked. Up until the early 1980s many art therapists were based in occupational therapy departments and their work was part of the overall service provided by them. Though this is no longer the case, many art therapists continue to work alongside occupational therapists on a day-to-day basis. Secondly, there is a long history of occupational therapists using art 'as a therapeutic modality in mental health' (Lloyd and Papas, 1999: 31). This includes the use of projective techniques as an aid to diagnosis (Alleyne, 1980; Monroe and Herron, 1980) through to the use of art to foster self-awareness and communication (Brock, 1991; Dollin, 1976; Frye, 1990).

Although the use of art in mental health settings by occupational therapists appears to have declined since the mid-1980s, a trend, in part, influenced by the development of art therapy as a profession, their work in this area is nevertheless frequently confused with that undertaken by art therapists. It may, therefore, be helpful to examine the areas of commonality and difference between the two professions in order to clarify further what art therapy is, as well as what it is not. In their discussion of this issue, Atkinson and Wells (2000: 20) identify four main areas of difference between art therapy and the use of art in occupational therapy. These they distinguish as, education and training, the use of a single arts based medium, the importance attached to the artwork, and the level of direction evident within the therapeutic approach.

Education and training
Art therapy training takes place at postgraduate level, with the vast majority of art therapists already possessing an undergraduate degree in a related

subject; usually fine art. This is not the case for occupational therapists whose basic training is at undergraduate level.

The use of a single arts based medium

Art therapy is primarily concerned with the therapeutic application of one or more of the visual arts such as painting, drawing or sculpture. In addition to the experience and understanding of these gained prior to and during their training many art therapists are actively involved with the medium of art outside their work. Indeed, this is widely regarded as essential if art therapists are to remain in touch with the discipline upon which their clinical practice is based (Gilroy, 1989; Moon, 2001). Occupational therapists, by contrast, often use a wide range of arts based media (drama, creative writing, music, as well as paper and paint) in their work and few would claim to possess any specialist skills in these disciplines.

The importance attached to the artwork

By and large, occupational therapists tend to place far less emphasis on the artwork than would an art therapist. For art therapists product and process are integral to one another, whereas in occupational therapy the finished artwork is generally regarded as being of secondary importance to the therapeutic process; the primary aim being to gain information about the client through observing their engagement with their artwork (Patrick and Winship, 1994).

The level of direction evident within the therapeutic approach

Although some art therapists may suggest themes for clients to work to, most tend not to plan sessions or provide specific directions as to how the available materials should be used. Whereas an occupational therapist might, for example, attach considerable importance to the use of a particular medium in a session art, therapists generally prefer to offer clients a free choice.

Variations on a Theme: The Title Debate

Another difficulty in distinguishing art therapy from other forms of art based therapeutic intervention concerns the range of titles under which art therapists now practice. There are two important aspects to this. Firstly, and often for historical reasons, in various non-clinical settings such as prisons or in social services, the title under which an art therapist is employed may vary. It is not uncommon for an art therapist working in a prison to be called an 'art tutor' or a 'group worker' in social service establishments. Secondly, and to further complicate matters, in the early 1990s there was considerable debate within the profession in the UK concerning whether or not practitioners should change their title from art therapist to art psychotherapist. Some art therapists expressed the view that the term 'art therapy' no longer adequately reflected the psychotherapeutic nature of the work undertaken by art therapists (Dudley and Mahoney, 1991; Waller, 1989). In opposition to these views, other art therapists argued that a change of title might result in the loss of a unique professional identity and that by being linked with verbally based psychotherapy there would be a consequent loss of emphasis on the power of the creative process in art therapy (Thomson, 1992). It is interesting to note that similar disputes and debates have surfaced periodically in the USA and 'continue to contribute to the liveliness of the field' (Junge and Asawa, 1994: 31).

Although the membership of the British Association of Art Therapists voted to retain the title art therapist, albeit narrowly, what emerged very clearly during this period was the plural nature of the profession. This diversity of approach within art therapy is reflected in the proliferation of titles under which members of the profession now practice. In addition to art therapist and art psychotherapist, these now include analytical art psychotherapist (Schaverien, 1994), group analytic art therapist (McNeilly, 1984) and person-centred art therapist (Silverstone, 1997). In the USA, the range of titles under which art therapists practice is even more extensive and includes cognitive, gestalt, medical, phenomenological and studio approaches to art therapy; see Junge and Asawa (1994) and Rubin (1999, 2001). The emergence of these different titles and approaches to art therapy has been determined by a number of factors, including the context in which art therapy takes place, the client group with whom the art therapist works and the art therapist's theoretical orientation. As a consequence, art therapy has come to mean different things to different people. Indeed, as Watkins (1981: 107) observes, there exists no natural kinship between therapists who depend upon images for their theories or therapeutic techniques, 'Nor does the founding of a single kind of therapy (for instance art therapy or sand play therapy) coalesce its group of practitioners. Within it there will be radical differences in approach to the imaginal'. Given the potential these different theoretical positions and ways of working have for generating disagreement and fragmentation, it is a remarkable fact that art therapy in the UK has developed as a coherent and unified profession.

Why Art Therapy?

Although human communication may take many forms, in a society such as ours words tend to dominate. Not only are words the main means by which we exchange information about the world in which we live, but words are, for most people, the main means they have available for expressing and communicating their experience of that world. It is through words that most of us, in our daily lives at least, attempt to shape and give meaning to experience. Human experience cannot, however, be entirely reduced to words. Expressing how it feels to love or hate, to be traumatised or to suffer depression may involve far more than struggling to find the 'right' words. Some experiences and emotional states are beyond words. This is particularly relevant where difficulties originate in early infancy, a time when we experience the world in advance of any ability to describe it in words. It is here that art therapy offers a way of overcoming the frustration, terror and isolation such experiences may engender, by providing an alternative medium for expression and communication through which feelings might be conveyed and understood.

Art therapy may prove helpful to people with a wide range of needs and difficulties for a number of reasons.

In the context of a supportive relationship making images, and thinking and feeling in images, which among other things involves the use of the imagination and the taking of risks, can further a person's emotional growth, self-esteem, psychological and social integration.

'Sam'

I had heard of Sam long before I first met him. He was widely known as 'The Artist' within the hospital I had recently begun working in, and someone I ought, therefore, to meet. When we did eventually meet, Sam was very keen to show me his work and how it was made. Sam had spent many years in prison, during which time he had developed a highly personal way of working using the very limited materials available to him.

Using any flat surface with a texture, wax crayons, boot polish and an implement with a flat edge (in demonstrating his technique to me he used a clay modelling tool) Sam was able to create enormously subtle images in which figure or figures and background intermingled with a dream-like intensity. Sam evidently experienced considerable satisfaction in being able to produce such images at will, but expressed little interest in discussing their personal significance. It was to be very much later in our relationship before he felt able to share with me the story and circumstances that led him to begin making images. It appeared to be enough that he could make them and that doing so afforded him an established identity as an artist.

Over time, however, it became increasingly apparent that Sam's work showed no signs of change or development. Indeed he was

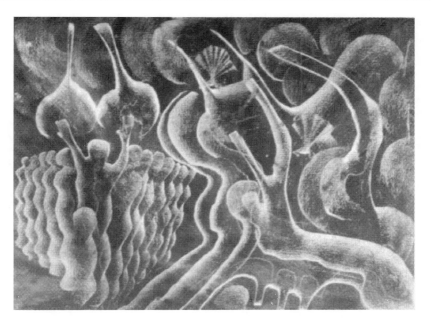

1.2   Sam

frequently unable to make images. At such times he often complained of feeling 'empty inside' and would drink heavily to dull the pain or in search of inspiration. When Sam was able to make images, he tended to repeat the same mechanical gestures, and use the same formulaic shapes, over and over again. Moreover, there seemed to be no connection between the images he made and how he felt or what difficulties preoccupied him at the time. It was as though Sam's creativity had become restricted by his own style of image making. The fact that his identity as a person, and much of his self-esteem, was bound up with being an artist who produced such unusual images made it very difficult for Sam to develop new or different ways of working. To do so was too great a risk to take.

Gradually, Sam did begin to experiment with his image making. Having become a regular visitor to the art therapy department, he became increasingly confident in his use of a wide range of different media and materials. Sam was also able to draw upon the support offered to risk sharing his thoughts and feelings, both through his images and through his relationships with others.

Through making images and objects it is possible to externalise and objectify experience so that it becomes possible to reflect upon it.

'Brenda'

Brenda found her way to art therapy following a referral by her psychiatrist. In the months preceding her admission to hospital, Brenda had become increasingly anxious and had made repeated visits to her GP complaining of various illnesses for which no physical cause could be found. It was felt that art therapy might help Brenda find less disabling ways of expressing her feelings and gain some insight into her difficulties. Brenda's referral was unusual in that unlike the majority of clients seen in art therapy she was an accomplished graphic artist. Although this made her a very obvious candidate for art therapy, to begin with Brenda actually found it extremely difficult to use her skills to give form to her feelings. Brenda's early drawings were little different in style or content to those she contributed to various magazines from time to time.

On one occasion, however, Brenda showed me a series of drawings she had produced as illustrations for a Russian folk tale, the Baba Yaga (see Figure 1.3).

In this story a young girl is sent by her stepmother to live with her aunt, an evil witch who is cruel and wants to eat her up. The young heroine eventually escapes this fate through acts of kindness and, reunited with her father at the end of the story, lived on and flourished.[1] As Brenda told me the tale of the Baba Yaga it seemed to me that there were some parallels between her own life experiences and those of the young heroine. Her mother was often portrayed in witch-like terms, and as someone who wished her dead. Having lost her father in childhood, Brenda also longed for a father figure who would rescue her. Once made, this link between the story of the Baba Yaga and her own story opened up the possibility for Brenda to begin making images that depicted events in her own life. To begin with she was able to do so only tentatively. Later, and with growing self-assurance, feelings Brenda found so difficult to articulate through words increasingly began to find expression through her images.

Over time, a number of themes emerged in Brenda's artwork. These included her fear of rejection and humiliation, along with feelings of helplessness and dependence. Above all, Brenda's images began to convey some of the intense frustration and rage she felt in relation to her

1.3   Brenda

boyfriend, mother and sisters, by whom she often felt belittled and per-
secuted. This was a huge step for Brenda to take, as all her life she had
been actively discouraged from expressing her anger. Through her art-
work Brenda was able to reconnect with areas of her emotional life
from which she had long felt alienated. Expressing how she felt, rather
than suppressing, this also enabled Brenda to begin to assert her own
needs and take control of her own life.

For some clients the images and objects they create may help to hold or
contain feelings that might otherwise be experienced as unbearable.

'Rita'

Rita was a deeply troubled woman with a complex array of physical
and psychological problems. Periodically admitted to hospital after
having become overwhelmed by fears and delusions, Rita lived in an

1.4 Brenda

in-between world. Unable to fend for herself in the outside world, she also hated the restrictions being in hospital imposed upon her life. Following her discharge from hospital Rita craved the sanctuary institutional life offered her and frequently precipitated crises that led to her readmission. In art therapy, this ambivalence expressed itself through her erratic attendance and tendency to idealise or denigrate others, including myself. Rita's inclination to divide her world into good and bad found expression in the very different kinds of images she produced. Her images depicted the world or people, including herself, as good or bad. One day, however, Rita produced an image that marked a significant departure from this pattern (see Figure 1.5).

For the first time in art therapy, Rita was able to create an image that expressed her mixed feelings about herself and her struggle to live independently. The particular significance of this image only became apparent much later in art therapy when she felt safe enough to begin to explore the terror she felt in relation to being unable to separate from her mother. The importance this image had at the time it was made,

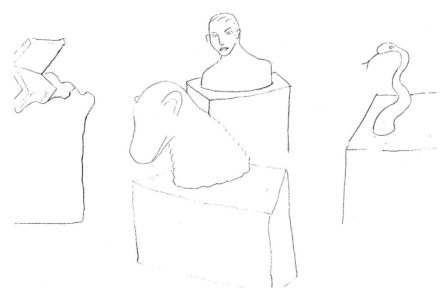

1.5   Rita

however, lay in its capacity to contain and hold the ambivalent feelings she had hitherto experienced as unbearable and inexpressible. No longer entirely stuck or frozen within her, these feelings were now outside herself, contained within the borders of the sheet of paper on which they had been depicted.

It is through symbols that we are able to give shape or form to our experience of the world. This may provide the basis for self-understanding and emotional growth.

'Lily'

Made at the very end of art therapy Lily's image carried a number of very personal symbolic meanings. Firstly, it referred to the many tears Lily had shed during her life and over the course of therapy. Less overtly, the eye also referred to her wish to be seen. As a quiet, obedient child, Lily had been an almost invisible member of her family. Although Lily had developed this survival strategy to protect herself, her invisibility left her feeling uncared for. However, while Lily longed to be looked at, she was also terrified that if seen she would be rejected. This conflict, between seeing and being seen, had played a central role in art therapy. Lily's final image was so important

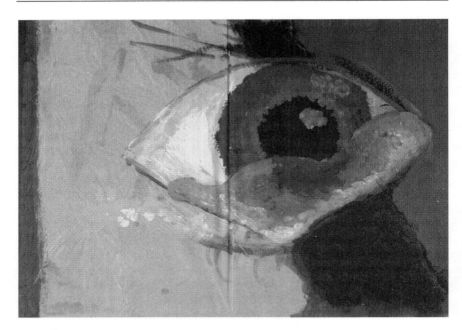

1.6 Lily

> *to her because while making it she came to recognise that seeing and being seen now felt safe and her fear of judgement had been replaced by feelings of self-acceptance.*

The physical nature of an artwork, for example, the way line, colour or shape are employed, provides a lasting record of the imaginative processes that produced it. Moreover, the permanence of art works – as contrasted to the transitory nature of verbal expression – may be especially useful in enabling the art therapist and the individuals with whom they work to follow and reflect upon changes occurring during the course of therapy. This helps establish a sense of focus and continuity that might otherwise be lost or prove difficult to maintain.

'Pete'

> *Pete was referred for art therapy because he found it difficult to talk about his problems. He had been diagnosed as suffering from depression and had been drinking heavily prior to his admission to hospital. At the beginning of art therapy Pete was very withdrawn. He also found it difficult to engage with the art materials. His first images were messy, fragmented and apparently lacking*

1.7 Pete (detail)

coherence. Pete seemed to be making these doodle-like images simply to pass the time. It was noticeable, however, that the cartoon character Snoopy would put in an occasional appearance (see Figure 1.7).

It was only much later in art therapy, after he had begun to make images in which Snoopy played a more prominent role that the significance of this became apparent. Pete identified himself with Snoopy. So much so, in fact, that he had a tattoo of Snoopy on his upper arm. Once I was aware of this it was possible for Pete and me to review his earlier work with this identification in mind. Earlier images, which appeared at the time to be devoid of emotion or personal meaning, could be seen in a new light. That is, as tentative attempts to locate himself in and through his images. The appearance of Snoopy in images made at different times also helped us both to see more clearly the process of change, both in Pete's images and in himself.

1.8 Pete

Although the forgoing vignettes are intended to give an indication of the ways in which art therapy may help individuals with a variety of problems, these examples are by no means exhaustive. The aims of art therapy will inevitably vary according to the needs of the individual or client group, and these may range from encouraging personal autonomy and self-motivation, to working with fantasy material and the unconscious (Liebmann, 1981). It is also necessary to acknowledge that for some clients making images can pose the threat of an embarrassing or destructive experience and may be resisted or avoided, irrespective of its potential benefits. This issue is explored more fully in Chapter 4.

Client groups

The range of settings in which art therapists now work is extensive and constantly developing. These include hospitals, schools, community-based centres, therapeutic communities and prisons. Art therapy is also often included as part of the services provided to particular client groups such as children, adolescents, families, older adults and individuals with learning difficulties. Within these broad areas art therapists may work with individuals on a one-to-one basis or with groups. Art therapists are also to be found practicing in a number of specialist fields including work with offenders, clients who have autism, eating disorders, addictions or who have experienced physical or sexual abuse, psychosis and physical illnesses. Increasingly, art therapists are also to be found working privately as well as in the public sector.

Note

1. A version of this story can be found in *The Virago Book of Fairy Tales* (Carter, 1991).

2

THE HISTORICAL BACKGROUND TO ART THERAPY

Precursors

The idea that a picture or object might have psychological importance for its creator, aside from whatever aesthetic qualities it may possess, is one we nowadays almost take for granted. When we look at a young child's drawing, discover ourselves doodling during a particularly dull meeting, or are presented with a pile of quickly rendered images by a visibly distressed client, we recognise that these images have meaning even if we do not always know how to 'read' or understand them. That we attribute meaning to such creations, and take seriously the healing potential of art, is due to a number of factors. M. Edwards (1989) suggests these include:

- The use of art in religious and spiritual practices.
- Philosophical debates about the relationship between creativity and madness.
- Developments in the visual arts.
- The 'discovery' of 'outsider' art and the art of the insane.
- The belief that the arts have a key role to play in promoting intellectual and emotional development.
- And the development of psychological theories that placed a positive value on dreaming, fantasising, playing and other forms of imaginative activity such as drawing or painting.

Taken together, these ideas and beliefs have reshaped the way we look at art, both inside and outside the gallery. Of particular importance in the development of art therapy has been the manner in which art, psychiatry and psychoanalysis combined in a variety of ways to provide the conditions out of which the profession emerged during the 1940s.

Art Historical Influences

While the term 'art therapy' may be one of fairly recent origin, interest in the expressive, psychological and potentially healing power of art has a much longer history. Indeed, it might well be argued that the roots of art therapy stretch back into prehistory, to a time when people first began to make images and objects intended to influence, make sense of, or express their experience. Throughout time, and across the globe, countless examples can be found of the use of the visual arts in healing rituals. Although the beliefs and practices embodied in prehistoric art, religious and healing rituals may be said to provide the distant cultural backdrop out of which art therapy eventually emerged (McNiff, 1979), it was to be the radical and momentous changes concerning the nature and function of art that took place in the second half of the nineteenth century that were to prove particularly significant.

Romanticism

It was during the Romantic period that the visual arts became markedly less concerned with the depiction of external reality, and more directly with subjectivity and self-expression (Vaughan, 1995). As a cultural movement, Romanticism arose in response to the rationalism and physical materialism of the Enlightenment. Among the characteristic attitudes of Romanticism were a deepened appreciation of nature, the privileging of emotion over reason, a turning in upon the self and a heightened examination of human personality; especially that of the genius and the hero. As Hughes (1981: 269) observes, 'One of the great themes of nineteenth-century romantic painting was the interplay between the world and the spirit: the search for images of those states of mind, embodied in nature, that exist beyond or below our conscious control'. Given the Romantic preoccupation with extreme or heightened emotional states, it is hardly surprising that madness itself became a major theme of nineteenth-century Romantic painting as found in the work of artists such as Fuseli, Goya and Gericault. Commenting on this trend MacGregor states,

> Madness held within it the promise of new and unexplored realms of the imagination, and the Romantic artist constantly seems to have felt that another world lay just inches away, that he was separated from it by the thinnest of membranes, and that some sudden turn of the mind could lead him, all unresisting, into this unexplored, and vastly more real, reality. (1989: 76)

In the late nineteenth, and early twentieth century, the Romantic interest in the exploration and representation of extreme emotional states surfaces in the work of artists such as van Gogh and Edvard Munch and in that of Expressionist painters including Kirchner, Nolde and Kandinsky (Dube, 1972; Selz, 1974).

Expressionism

A central feature of expressionist painting is the representation of emotion in its most immediate and compelling form. To achieve these ends, the subject is frequently exaggerated, distorted, or otherwise altered in order to stress the artist's emotional relationship with both the subject matter and medium. The influence of the expressionist impulse on the history of art in general, and art therapy in particular, has been extensive, most notably in the emphasis placed on originality and self-expression. Moreover, the self-conscious application of crude brush strokes, shape, colour and texture left in its wake an extensive visual language through which emotional states could be expressed and communicated without reference to narrative or the faithful representation of external reality. In the search to break free from the traditions of the past, and find new ways of giving form to inner experience, Expressionist artists drew inspiration from a wide variety of sources, but particularly from 'primitive' art forms such as those found in the art of the European Middle Ages, non-European cultures, folk art and the art of children. As Rhodes (1994: 9) observes, 'The primitive was regarded, on the whole, as always more instinctive, less bound by artistic convention and history, and somehow closer to fundamental aspects of human existence'. Unfortunately, this perspective contains within it a number of enduring, even racist, assumptions about the nature of 'primitive' societies, which are often perceived as uncivilised or childlike. It has also helped 'create a picture of primitive peoples as savage and illogical, acting without awareness or reflection, being directed by their unconscious drives' (Tipple, 1995: 11).

Interest in art forms existing outside familiar or accepted cultural norms also led to a developing awareness of the art of the insane. This interest moved in two principal directions; the medical and the artistic. Of particular importance in re-evaluating the aesthetic and creative significance of the art of the mentally ill was the German psychiatrist and art historian Hans Prinzhorn.

Prinzhorn and 'The Artistry of the Mentally Ill'

Prinzhorn, who was aware of the formal similarities to be found in both expressionist art and the art of the mentally ill, was particularly interested in the origins of the artistic impulse and hoped to further his understanding of this through the study of art works produced by psychiatric patients. Between 1880–1920, with the support of Karl Wilmanns, the head of the Psychiatric Department in Heidelberg, Prinzhorn built up a unique collection of works produced in institutions and asylums throughout the German-speaking world (Busine et al., 1998).[1] The majority of these patients, many of whom had been hospitalised for years on end, were diagnosed as schizophrenic. In 1922 Prinzhorn published *The Artistry of the Mentally Ill* (Prinzhorn, 1995) in which many of the works in the collection were illustrated and discussed in terms of their having recognisable artistic quality. Prinzhorn identified six basic psychological drives or urges that in his view determined the nature of the 'pictorial configurations' he studied. These he described as the expressive urge, the urge to play, the ornamental urge, the ordering tendency, the tendency to imitate and the need for symbols. Through choosing to study and write about the art of the mentally ill from an artistic, rather than a medical perspective, Prinzhorn gave this marginalised form of art, and its creators, a positive re-evaluation. According to MacGregor (1989: 5) Prinzhorn's importance to the study and appreciation of art produced by the mentally ill was that he 'forced the recognition that there was no psychopathology of art or expression'. MacGregor continues,

> Man's images, to the extent that they embody and communicate human reality, however strange or pathological that reality may be, belong firmly and without qualification to that sequence of unforgettable images to which we give the name art. (1989: 5)

This view has not found universal acceptance. Nor has Prinzhorn's assertion that no useful purpose would be served by comparing the art of schizophrenics and contemporary art. In Prinzhorn's opinion, to do so 'would serve only to arm the philistines with fresh platitudes' (1995: 271). His work did, however, give authority to the view that the art produced by the mentally ill could be understood as a means of counteracting the most extreme forms of psychological and social isolation.

Outsider Art

The publication of *The Artistry of the Mentally Ill* was enthusiastically received and almost immediately found an audience beyond psychiatry. This audience included many prominent avant-garde artists of the period. Particularly affected by the work illustrated and discussed in Prinzhorn's book was the French artist Jean Dubuffet. Immediately after World War Two, Dubuffet began to collect unusual works by psychiatric patients and other untrained artists whose creativity owed little to art history or contemporary culture.[2] Dubuffet applied the term 'Art Brut' (Raw Art) to this form of art because it was uncooked by culture and represented art in its rawest and purest state. For Dubuffet, culture was the enemy of true creativity. The commonest English-language equivalent for Art Brut is 'outsider art', whereas in North America the same phenomenon tends to attract the label 'grass-roots art' (see Cardinal, 1972; Maizels, 1996; Rhodes, 2000).[3] Outsider art has played an important role in the development of art therapy, primarily through its influence on many of the early art therapists. As Waller (1991: 27) comments, many of these found their way into art therapy 'through an initial fascination with the paintings of psychiatric patients they had seen in the various exhibitions of the late 1950s and early 1960s'.

Surrealism

The inward looking trend evident in both Romanticism and Expressionism resurfaces in the work of the Surrealists. Surrealism, the artistic and literary movement founded by André Breton in 1924, celebrated the unconscious as a liberating force and regarded it as the source of an art devoid of the degenerating effects of rationality. The Surrealists drew inspiration from a wide range of sources, including 'primitive' and 'outsider' art.

> Here there was an inexhaustible reservoir of authentic works, motivated neither by a desire to please, nor by material interest, nor by artistic ambition, but by the irrepressible need to pour out a message from the depths of the being. (Alexandrian, 1995: 25)

In their search for an art able to fully exploit the power of the mind to produce seemingly irrational imagery, as in the startling or incongruous juxtapositions of objects to be found in dreams, the Surrealists also began to quarry the work and ideas of Sigmund Freud. André Breton defined Surrealism as,

> Pure psychic automatism, by which it is intended to express, verbally, in writing, or by other means, the real process of thought. Thought's dictation in the absence of all control exercised by the reason outside all aesthetic or moral preoccupations. (Breton in Chipp, 1973: 412)

Thus, at the very heart of one of the twentieth century's most influential forms of artistic practice, we have in all but name Freud's concept of 'free association'. Free association being the mode of spontaneous thinking encouraged in the patient by the analyst's injunction that they obey the basic rule of psychoanalysis and report all thoughts without self-censorship.[4] This technique is based on the premise that all lines of thought lead to what is significant and that resistance to unconscious thoughts or feelings entering consciousness is minimised by relaxation.

> The Surrealists thought no aesthetic accident, no simple act of spilling paint, no visual juxtaposition – however irrational – as psychoanalytically, and therefore artistically, irrelevant. Indeed the abstract, accidental, and often illegible marks

created through automatism could themselves elicit visual images, which in turn would be elaborated on, albeit in an obviously conscious and more premeditated fashion. (Cernuschi, 1992: 4–5)

Pure psychic automatism is best exemplified in the automatic drawings of André Masson and the frottage works of Max Ernst. Within art therapy free association and 'pure psychic automatism' find their equivalent in the emphasis placed on spontaneous painting and modelling.

Despite the inspiration his pioneering work undoubtedly provided for them, the ends towards which the Surrealists applied Freud's clinical technique and theories were very different to those of psychoanalysis. Whereas psychoanalysis aimed to alleviate mental and emotional distress, Surrealism was primarily concerned with social revolution and liberating the human imagination. The Surrealists wished to exploit the irrationality of the unconscious to reach 'a reality beyond perceptible or rational proof' (Duro and Greenhalgh, 1993: 281). If the Surrealists sought to esteem the 'exotic', 'primitive', 'bizarre' and the 'mad', for Freud, neurosis was an illness, a condition to be cured, not celebrated. It is perhaps not surprising, therefore, to discover that Freud tended to view the Surrealist enterprise with a degree of coolness and scepticism. Nevertheless, it might also be argued that the duel aims of alleviating emotional distress and liberating the imagination are far from being incompatible. Indeed both underpin the clinical practice of art therapy.

The Influence of Psychiatry

Before discussing the influence of psychiatry on the development of art therapy, it is first of all necessary to acknowledge that the ways in which societies have understood and responded to madness have changed considerably over time (Ellenberger, 1994; Porter, 2002). Behaviour once viewed as evidence of demonic possession, or due to an imbalance of 'the humours', has subsequently been perceived as arising out of a disordered imagination, a disease of the brain or, more recently, from a genetic predisposition, psychological trauma or a biochemical imbalance affecting the mind (Alexander and Selesnick, 1967; Shorter, 1997). Each of these different perspectives on 'madness' embodies a range of assumptions about human nature, human suffering and about the solutions to that suffering. At the present time, and especially in western industrialised societies, the dominant view of madness is that it is a biologically based illness requiring medical intervention, usually through the use of psychiatric medication.

The process by which madness came to be redefined as an illness, and hence as a condition almost exclusively within the remit of the medical profession, remains contentious and beyond the scope of this book (see Scull (1981, 1993) and Szasz (1974, 1977) for a detailed discussion of this issue).[5] The fact remains, however, that for well over a century psychiatrists have presided over the care and treatment of the mentally disordered. For art therapy the influence of psychiatry has been most evident in the therapeutic application of art in mental health care and in the use of art as an aid to diagnosis.

The Therapeutic Application of Art in Mental Health Care

From the mid-1700s onwards, the view that lunacy was the result of a bodily disease began to assert itself. The lunatic came to be seen as human, albeit that he or she was perceived as lacking self-control or the capacity to reason. Institutions for the treatment and rehabilitation, as opposed to the incarceration, of the insane began to be built and more humane methods of treating mental illness were pioneered by individuals such as Phillipe Pinel in France, William Tuke in England and Dorothea Dix in the USA. This approach came to be referred to as 'moral treatment' and initially consisted of the simple, yet profound, step of substituting compassion and gentleness for cruelty and brutality. The therapeutic regimes that developed in these asylums included exercise, work and other forms of occupation (Paterson, 2002). There was also, as Hogan (2001: 41) observes, a growing realisation that art was valuable in rehabilitating a patient's mental health, not as 'a mere distraction, but rather as a tool in the acquisition of self-control, and as a means to the elevation of the spirit'. Though some advocates of moral treatment argued that the uninhibited expression of the imagination could be detrimental, others maintained that art helped 'impart healthy vigour to the body and ... that tranquillity which allows and facilitates the operation of rebuke, remonstrance, threats, encouragement or reasoning' (Dr W.A.F Browne (1841) quoted in Hogan, 2001: 42).

The idea that the mentally ill might benefit from understanding and compassion was further developed by later physicians, especially in Europe. As MacGregor observes:

> Out of the Romantic preoccupation with introspection, the irrational, and the more private and intense emotions, came insights into the depths of the mind; the discovery of the unconscious and its profound role in the life of the individual, and an understanding of the role of psychological conflict in the genesis of mental disturbance. (1989: 187)

The first half of the nineteenth century saw the development of psychologically-based methods of treatment, including early forms of verbal psychotherapy, and the 'first hints that music, art and drama were useful therapeutic expressions in the treatment of hospitalised mental patients' (MacGregor, 1989: 187). One of the most influential figures during this period was the German psychiatrist Johann Reil, who is now regarded as one of the founders of modern psychiatry. In his treatise *Rhapsodies on the application of the psychic cure method*, published in 1803, Reil outlines an elaborate programme for the treatment of mental illness that included 'the use of "therapeutic theatre", work, exercises and art therapy' (cited in Ellenberger, 1994: 212). The aim of this programme being to uncover and release those hidden passions Reil believed caused mental disorder (Casson, 2001).

Influential though such pioneering developments were in promoting more humane forms of treatment, as psychiatry moved closer to medicine the view that mental illness was the result of a brain abnormality gradually came to assert itself. Henceforth, the structure and workings of the brain became the focus of psychiatric investigation and treatment. Among the many consequences of this were the increasing emphasis placed upon physical, rather than psychological, forms of treatment (including electro convulsive therapy, psycho-surgery and medication) and the isolation of the mentally ill in vast asylums. Sadly, as the asylums became ever larger and more costly to run, conditions became poor, therapeutic contact limited and the problems associated with institutionalisation began to manifest themselves (Goffman, 1973; Jones and Fowles, 1984). Moreover, the therapeutic potential of the visual arts were largely relegated to a supplementary role, often in the form of diversional, recreational or educational activities. Nevertheless, it was to be against this background, and within these psychiatric institutions, that art therapy began to emerge in the UK as a distinct profession from the late 1940s onwards.

Diagnostic Approaches to the Art of the Insane

The triumph of medical psychiatry did little to foster greater understanding of the symbolic and therapeutic value of the art produced by the mentally ill. The belief that brain abnormality might be revealed through drawing or painting did, however, result in a renewed interest in the diagnostic potential of art. Although artworks created by individuals deemed mad had long been collected as curiosities, it was not until the end of the nineteenth century that physicians, including the French psychiatrists Ambroise Tardieu and Max Simon, began to consider the relevance these images and objects might have for the individuals who created them. Perhaps the best known of these figures is the Italian psychiatrist Cesare Lombroso, whose study of the relationship between madness and creativity *L'uomo di genio* (Man of Genius), published in 1882, was hugely influential in establishing the myth that mental instability and genius were inextricably linked. As Cardinal (1972: 16) comments, 'the equation 'genius = madness' passed into common currency with alarming speed, and even now many people imagine that the force of Van Gogh's later work can be explained simply in terms of his mental breakdown'.

The trend towards the description and classification of mental illness pioneered by psychiatrists such as Emil Kraepelin and Eugen Bleuler during the late nineteenth and early twentieth century led to a renewed interest in the artworks produced by the mentally ill. This interest being primarily concerned with the ways in which disturbances in thinking revealed through image making might be used for diagnostic purposes. An early pioneer in this area was the German psychiatrist Fritz Mohr, who devised an experimental procedure for studying the drawings of mentally ill patients with the intention of relating these to specific types of neurological dysfunction. The procedure devised by Mohr included requesting that the patient copy simple drawings, drawing anything that occurred to them and completing unfinished drawings (see MacGregor, 1989: 190). In adopting this approach, Mohr anticipated many of the visually-based psychological tests still in use today such as the 'House-Tree-Person' projective drawing technique (Blain et al., 1981; Buck, 1992) and the Draw-A-Person-Test (Culbertson and Revel, 1987). When using the House-Tree-Person test, for example, the client is asked to draw a picture of a house, a tree, and a person. Once completed, the client is then asked to tell a story related to each picture. The H-T-P and other similar projective tests are based on the belief that what the client paints or draws will reflect aspects of the personality that might be otherwise unavailable to consciousness or for assessment (see Chapter 7).[6]

Though questions remain regarding the validity and reliability of many of the measures used in art based assessment tests such as the H-T-P test (Hacking and Foreman, 2001; Trowbridge, 1995), their use has played a significant role in the development of art therapy. It is necessary to acknowledge here that although art therapists in the UK do not routinely use art for diagnostic purposes, in the US the position is very different. This difference may largely be explained by the fact that due to the nature of health care delivery systems in the USA, there is, as Gilroy and Skaife (1997: 60) note, a direct 'correlation between diagnosis and the kind of treatments which will be financed by insurance companies'. Gilroy and Skaife continue,

> The fact that diagnosis is linked so directly to the funding of particular treatment programmes has a profound effect on American art therapy practice: diagnosis is central to the initiation of any treatment plan, hence the American art therapists' emphasis on their diagnostic skills. (1997: 60)

In the UK, it has been psychiatrists, rather than art therapists, who have used art for research and diagnostic purposes. The key figures in the psychiatric study of art were the émigré psychiatrists Erich Guttmann, Walter Mayer-Gross and Francis Reitman, who had moved to the UK following the rise of Nazism in Europe, and the Scottish psychiatrist Walter Maclay. From the late 1930s onwards these psychiatrists collaborated on a series of research projects at the Maudsley Hospital in London concerned with visual and self-perception in 'depersonalisation' and 'manic depressive psychosis' (Waller, 1991: 28). In order to extend their research they also began to acquire and collect images produced by psychiatric patients (particularly those diagnosed as schizophrenics and patients who had undergone psycho-surgery) as well as 'normal' subjects.

As Hogan (2001: 164) observes, the primary focus of this research became the study of 'how schizophrenic patients perceive and express change in themselves pictorially during the course of their illness'. As with so many other enquiries of this kind, however, the visual image was essentially regarded as a depiction of psychopathology. The meaning attached to these images by the individuals who created them was of lesser concern.

Edward Adamson

In 1945 Reitman moved to the Netherne Hospital in Surrey where he worked with another psychiatrist, Eric Cunningham Dax. Cunningham Dax shared Reitman's interest in the art of psychiatric patients, but did so more out of an appreciation of its therapeutic potential, particularly as a means of providing emotional release. This interest in the therapeutic application of art appears to have been influenced by the development of the therapeutic community for the psychiatric rehabilitation of servicemen at Northfield Military Hospital in Birmingham. According to Waller (1991: 30) Cunningham Dax visited Northfield and, impressed with what he saw, including a painting group, 'decided to introduce such a group at Netherne'. In 1946 the artist Edward Adamson was appointed to the role of 'art master' (Hogan, 2001: 170).[7]

The conditions of Adamson's appointment were strictly limited to helping the medical team obtain images for their research. His role at the Netherne Hospital was 'to stimulate and receive, not to teach, not to analyse, but to observe and never to touch the patients' paintings' (Cunningham Dax in Waller, 1991: 54). It was particularly important to both Cunningham Dax and Reitman that the artwork produced in Adamson's studio was obtained under experimental conditions and remained uncontaminated by any discussion of its symbolic content (Cunningham Dax, 1953; Reitman, 1950). This requirement appears to have dovetailed neatly with Adamson's own views on the interpretation of images. That either through encouragement or the desire to please, the artwork produced by patients would 'result in "Freudian phallic symbols or Jungian signs" depending on the theoretical orientation of the therapist' (Hogan, 2001: 175). Despite the initial restrictions imposed upon him, it is apparent from Adamson's own writing that he believed creativity to be inherently healing (Adamson, 1990). Adamson's non-interventionist approach exercised a significant influence on many later art therapists (Byrne, 1996; Hogan, 2000; Maclagan, 1984).

Psychoanalysis and Analytical Psychology

The third and, arguably, most significant influence upon the development of art therapy has been that exerted by psychoanalysis. Since Freud founded the profession, psychoanalysis has had much to say about the creative process, aesthetics and the interpretation of art. Indeed, all the major psychoanalytic schools have, from time to time, drawn upon the arts to support or substantiate their theories. Indeed, for many leading psycho-analysts, including Carl Jung (1969), Melanie Klein (1975), Donald Winnicott (1971), Marion Milner (1988) and Alice Miller (1996), painting and drawing often played an important role in their clinical work.

Sigmund Freud and Psychoanalysis

Freud's interest in art and creativity arose from his belief that neurotic symptoms developed as a consequence of the conflict between the pleasure and reality principles. For Freud the unconscious mental processes opera-tive in the neuroses, dreams, and the creation of works of art (including con-densation, displacement and symbolisation) functioned in similar ways. Freud termed this 'primary process' thinking. In contrast to this, mental functioning influenced by considerations of external reality Freud termed 'secondary process' thinking. The purpose of those forms of mental func-tioning Freud regarded as manifestations of the pleasure principle, such as play, day-dreaming and other forms of creative activity was to accumulate pleasure by re-arranging reality into new and more congenial forms. As Bateman and Holmes (1996: 129) comment, 'Freud seemed to believe that due to 'primal repression' some aspects of life could only be represented indirectly via symbols, thus putting repression and the potentiality for neurosis at the heart of dreaming, creativity and cultural life generally'.

Underlying Freud's approach to the neuroses, dreaming and creativity was his conviction that in order for an individual to adapt to the demands of external reality the imaginative processes operative in primary process thinking must be controlled or renounced. In adopting this perspective Freud further emphasises the well-established tendency in Western thought to favour reason over the expressive, intuitive and imaginative aspects of psychological life. In art, however, Freud saw a 'peculiar' reconciliation between the pleasure and reality principles. In his 1911 paper, 'Formulations on the Two Principles of Mental Functioning,' he wrote,

> An artist is originally a man who turns away from reality because he cannot come to terms with the renunciation of instinctual satisfaction which it at first demands, and who allows his erotic and ambitious wishes full play in the life of phantasy. He finds his way back to reality, however, from this world of phantasy by making use of special gifts to mould his phantasies into truths of a new kind, which are valued by men as precious reflections of reality. (Freud, 1975, vol. XII: 224).[8]

The term Freud introduced into the psychoanalytic vocabulary to describe the process by which the vestiges of infantile sexuality are transformed into socially valued forms like the creation of works of art was 'sublimation'.

Laplanche and Pontalis (1988: 431) define 'sublimation' as the 'process postulated by Freud to account for human activities which have no apparent connection with sexuality but which are assumed to be motivated by the force of the sexual instinct. The main types of activity described by Freud as sublimated are artistic creation and intellectual inquiry'.

What, in Freud's opinion, distinguishes the artist from the neurotic is that the former,

> understands how to work over his daydreams in such a way as to make them lose what is too personal about them and repels strangers, and to make it possible for others to share in the enjoyment of them. He understands, too, how to tone them down so that they do not easily betray their origin from proscribed sources. (Freud, 1975, vol. XVI: 376)

According to Freud, the means by which artists are able to do this is through a form of bribery. That is, 'by the purely formal ... aesthetic – yield of pleasure which he [the artist] offers us in the presentation of his phantasies' (Freud, 1975, vol. IX: 153).

One important consequence of Freud's approach to art has been to view it, like a dream or symptom, as the symbolic expression of the neurotic and conflicted inner world of the artist. Moreover, although Freud acknowledged that the experience of dreaming is predominantly visual, he was primarily concerned with translating dream imagery into words. Freud did, however, acknowledge the difficulty of doing this, 'Part of the difficulty of giving an account of dreams is due to our having to translate these images into words. "I could draw it", a dreamer often says to us, "but I don't know how to say it"' (Freud, 1979: 118). Dalley (1984: xvii) comments, 'One can only speculate on the impact of the development of art therapy had Freud permitted his patients to draw their dreams rather than tell them'.[9]

This split between process and product, and between words and images, is very evident in much of Freud's writing on visual art. See, for example, Freud's papers on Leonardo Da Vinci, 1910 and Michelangelo's Moses 1914 (Freud, 1975). Freud was primarily interested in the psychological content of art and appears to have had little appreciation for the manipulation of line, colour and form in painting, especially in non-figurative or expressionist painting. Fuller (1983: 5) reports that after an evening in the company of an artist Freud wrote disparagingly to his friend and colleague Ernest Jones '"Meaning is but little to these men all they care for is line, shape, agreement of contours. They are", he said, "given up to *lustprinzip*, or the pleasure principle"'. Nevertheless, the overall message conveyed through Freud's writing on art and artists is a positive, if at times ambivalent, one.

> Freud may have handled certain interpretative tasks roughly and been all but silent on certain artistic traditions and genres, but his overall message is surely encouraging: art is an enhancement of our lives, a partial taming of our savagery, and, although artists are propelled by passions that retain something of their primitive power and disruptiveness, the work they do on behalf of society is of an integrative and reparative kind. (Bowie, 1993: 56)

Carl Jung and Analytical Psychology

Carl Jung was a Swiss psychiatrist who became interested in psycho-analysis around the turn of the twentieth century. Jung visited Freud in Vienna in 1907 and a close friendship between the two men developed. This lasted until 1913 when personal and theoretical differences brought the relationship to an end and Jung left the psychoanalytic movement. From 1914 onwards, Jung used the term 'Analytical Psychology' to distinguish his ideas and method of working from those of Freud. The two approaches to understanding the complex, dynamic forces active in the inner world nevertheless share much common ground. While each may use different concepts and terminology, both approaches are grounded in the belief that our inner (subjective) life is determined by feelings, thoughts and impulses beyond conscious awareness but which may find expression in a symbolic form.

In a number of significant respects, however, Jung's approach to art and the imagination stands in marked contrast to that traditionally found in psychoanalysis. Following his break with Freud, Jung had a series of vivid, portentous dreams and fantasies. In order to better understand their significance, Jung wrote them down, later embellishing them with drawings. These writings and images are collected together in what is now known as the *Red Book* (Jung, 1985: 212–213). Unlike Freud, for whom psychoanalysis was a 'talking cure', Jung arrived at the view that it was through images that the most fundamental aspects of human experience and psychological life found expression. As a consequence, Jung fre-quently encouraged his patients to draw or paint as part of their analysis; see, for example, Jung's essays on 'The transcendent function' (Jung, 1969: 8) and 'A study in the process of individuation' (Jung, 1969: 9).

The pictures Jung's patients produced were seen as being of therapeutic value for two main reasons. Firstly, Jung believed they played a mediating role between the patient and his or her problem, and between the con-scious and unconscious mind. Secondly, image making provided the patient with an opportunity to externalise and thus establish some psy-chological distance from their difficulties. Thoughts and feelings experi-enced as unmanageable or chaotic could, through painting, be given form and expression. Jung's way of working with images was primarily aimed at encouraging an active relationship between the artist/patient and his or her imagery, rather than the production of further unconscious material for interpretation. The term Jung employed to describe this technique was 'active imagination' (Jung, 1997). The process of active imagination involves a particular kind of imaginative activity analogous to dreaming while awake,

> We have only to look at the drawings of patients who supplement their analysis by active imagination to see that colours are feeling values. Mostly, to begin with, only a pencil or pen is used to make rapid sketches of dreams, sudden ideas, and

fantasies. But from a certain moment ... the patients begin to make use of colour ... [and] merely intellectual interest gives way to emotional participation. (Jung, 1969, 14: paragraph 248)

The therapeutic value of this method is further emphasised by Jung's assertion that, 'Often the hands know how to solve a riddle with which the intellect has wrestled in vain' (Jung, 1997: 57).

An important reason Jung valued imaginative activity so highly is to be found in his understanding of the nature and function of symbols. For Freud, symbols, as found in dreams or art, were the expression of repressed, unconscious desires or wishes in a disguised form, whereas for Jung, 'The true symbol differs essentially from this, and should be understood as an intuitive idea that cannot yet be formulated in any other or better way' (Jung, 1969, 15: paragraph 105). Speaking of works of art that are openly symbolic, Jung states,

> Their pregnant language cries out to us that they mean more than they say. We can put our finger on the symbol at once, even though we may not be able to unriddle its meaning to our entire satisfaction. A symbol remains a perpetual challenge to our thoughts and feelings. That probably explains why a symbolic work is so stimulating, why it grips us so intensely, but also why it seldom affords us a purely aesthetic enjoyment. (Jung, 1969, 15: paragraph 119)

For Jung, symbolic forms have what he termed a 'transcendent function'. It is by means of symbolic forms that the transition from one psychological attitude or condition to another is affected. Through drawing on the archetypal patterns that Jung believed structured the human mind, each individual is regarded as having access to a rich store of images and narratives through which to give expression to conflicting aspects of the psyche. In Jungian theory, archetypes are, like the instincts, the inherited part of the psyche and belong to the collective unconscious (Fordham, 1973). Archetypes were said by Jung to cluster around the most fundamental and universal human life experiences – birth, parenthood, death and separation – and to reflect the structure of the psyche itself; revealing themselves by way of such inner figures as the 'anima', 'shadow' and 'persona'. As such, our dreams, fantasies and images all derive in part from a collective reservoir of symbols and myths that repeat themselves the world over (Jung, 1978).

An example of one such symbolic form frequently cited in the Jungian literature is the mandala (see Figure 2.1). Mandala is an ancient Sanskrit word meaning magic circle. Mandalas assume a variety of forms, but a basic mandala is a geometric figure in which a circle is squared or a square encircled.

Mandalas are found in the art of many religious traditions where they are employed in the service of personal growth and spiritual transformation. Tibetan Buddhism has employed mandalas for thousands of years as an aid to meditation and Navajo sand painters use them in healing rites. Jung considered the mandala to be an expression of the self and an archetypal symbol of wholeness (Samuels et al., 1986). Jung used the mandala as a

2.1 Mandala

therapeutic tool and believed creating mandalas helped patients to make the unconscious conscious. Examples of mandalas produced by patients of Jung can be found in *The Secret of the Golden Flower* (Jung, 1969: 13) and *A Study in the Process of Individuation* (Jung, 1969: 9).

The importance Jung attached to images and the imagination in psychological healing has had a marked influence on the development of art therapy. Maclagan comments,

> What made Jung a reference point for the later development of 'art therapy' was not just his insistence on the primacy of the image and the phantasy thinking that depends on it, nor the enormous importance he attached to archetypal symbolism, but his pioneering promotion of art making as an important path to psychological awareness. (2001: 85–86)

The attempts made by Jung and his followers to rescue art from the reductive scrutiny of psychoanalysis, and more specifically to challenge the view that creativity is synonymous with neurosis, has been highly influential within art therapy, particularly in the UK.

Notes

1. In its present form, the Prinzhorn collection consists of over 5,000 pieces of art, mainly drawings, paintings, collages, textiles, sculptures and writing. Further

information about the collection can be found at http://prinzhorn.uni-hd.de/im_ueberblick_eng.shtml

2. During his travels Dubuffet met the Swiss psychiatrist Dr Walter Morgenthaler who in 1921 published a book on the work of Adolf Wölfli, a 'schizophrenic' artist who produced a remarkable number of elaborate pencil drawings; see MacGregor (1989, Chapter 13).

3. In 1971 Dubuffet bequeathed the Collection de l'Art Brut to the City of Lausanne in Switzerland where it is now on permanent display to the public; see www.regart.ch/lausanne/art_brut/fra/index.asp?navig=1 Examples of contemporary Outsider Art can be found at www.rawvision.com

4. Laplanche and Pontalis (1988: 169) define free association as the 'method according to which voice must be given to all thoughts without exception which enter the mind, whether such thoughts are based upon a specific element (word, number dream-image or any kind of idea at all) or produced spontaneously'.

5. A useful history of mental health care can be found online at www.mdx.ac.uk/www/study/mhhtim.htm

6. Further information on the variety of art therapy assessment tools currently used for clinical and research purposes can be found at www.arttherapy.org/research/assessments.htm See also Rubin (1999), Chapter 7.

7. According to Hogan (2001: 170), a number of alternative titles were considered to define Adamson's role; including 'art teacher', 'art instructor', 'art occupationalist' and 'art therapist'. Both Adamson and Cunningham Dax appear, however, to have preferred the title 'the artist'.

8. In the psychoanalytic literature the word 'phantasy', is spelled with a 'ph' rather than with an 'f', in order to identify it as an unconscious mental process.

9. Interestingly, it is known that at least one of Freud's patients did draw their dreams. This image, and the dream it depicts, gave its name to one of Freud's most important case studies, that of the Wolf-Man (see Freud, 1975, vol. XVII: 30, Fig. 1).

3

THE EMERGENCE OF ART THERAPY AS A PROFESSION IN THE UK

The History of Art Therapy in the UK

As discussed in the previous chapter, the roots of art therapy are to be found in a broad range of ideas and practices concerned with understanding the nature of emotional distress and with the role of the visual arts in expressing or healing this. However, although the therapeutic potential of the visuals arts has a long history, the emergence of art therapy as a distinct profession is a relatively recent development. Wood suggests that the history of art therapy in the UK can be divided into three separate, but overlapping phases.

> During the first period, art therapists focused on the powerful means of expression they might offer to people with serious disorders and also on the provision of respectful containment. During the second period art therapists tried to counter some of the alienating effects of psychiatric institutions by providing an asylum within an asylum. In the third, contemporary, period the work of art therapists has become more influenced by psychotherapeutic practice … during this time questions of technique have become paramount. (Wood, 1997: 172)

Although Wood is writing primarily about the use of art therapy in relation to the treatment of psychosis, her schema can, I believe, be applied to the development of the profession as a whole.

Beginnings

The first period identified by Wood occurred between the 1940s and the late 1950s, during which time ideas about using art as therapy in hospital settings first emerged in a distinct and recognisable form. It was also during this period that the term art therapy began to be used with increasing frequency. However, as Hogan (2001: 186) observes, at this time 'Rather than being a distinct discipline, with clearly identifiable features, "art therapy" represented a variety of practices developing in specific contexts'.

A number of factors contributed to the emergence of art therapy during this period; most notably, the founding of the National Health Service in 1946 and the development of new approaches to the understanding and treatment of mental illness, including the founding of therapeutic communities and the widespread use of occupational and group therapies. Important though these developments were, it was largely as a consequence of the work of pioneer art therapists such as Adrian Hill (1948), Edward Adamson (1990), E.M. Lyddiatt (1971), Jan Glass (1963), Arthur Segal (1942), Joyce Laing (1984) and Rita Simon (1992; 1997) that the foundations of the profession were laid. These, and other less well known art therapists, did much to establish the credibility of art therapy and to draw its benefits to the attention of potential employers and the general public (see Waller, 1991 and Hogan, 2001).

The Influence of Art Education

Many of the early art therapists were artists and art teachers who, in developing their often very different approaches, drew upon an eclectic mix of ideas and personal experience. Of particular importance here was the kind of art education these early art therapists had themselves received, 'which in the 1940s and 1950s tended towards the "child-centred" approach' (Waller, 1991: 16). This approach to art education derives mainly from the work of Professor Franz Cizek who first used the term 'Child Art'. Cizek, who was appointed as head of the Department of Experimentation and Research at the Vienna School of Applied Arts in 1904, developed art-teaching methods that valued the child as an individual. Using Cizek's methods of teaching, children were encouraged to present, in visual form, their responses to events in their lives and develop personal methods of free expression rather than being subject to a rigid course of technical instruction. By this means, it was believed, the child's innate creativity could be fostered and thus aid emotional and intellectual development. In the UK the main proponent of child art and progressive methods of art teaching was Marion Richardson.

Marion Richardson was a prominent figure in art education during the 1930s and 1940s and was recognised by many of her contemporaries as revolutionary in her approach to art teaching. Richardson's work grew out of a technique of visualisation (the 'shut-eye' technique) that she believed would put children 'more in touch with their "inner world" and encourage spontaneous expression' (Waller, 1991: 20). This approach to art teaching was considered to have important implications for the personal as well as the artistic development of the children. Although the 'child-centred' approach to art education has largely fallen out of fashion in recent years, it was enormously influential at the time and many of the early art therapists had first hand experience of the teaching methods involved. Moreover, as Waller (1991: 16) suggests, 'the strong link with art education is peculiar to the development of art therapy in Britain and in the USA'.

The Promotion of Art Therapy

The promotional activities undertaken by the early pioneers of art therapy did much to attract later generations of art therapists to the profession. Diane Waller, who herself later became a key figure in the development of art therapy, recalls attending a lecture given by Edward Adamson in 1967 to accompany an exhibition of paintings by psychiatric patients from the Netherne Hospital.

> I was intrigued and excited by the paintings, curious about the people who had painted them, and curious about Adamson's approach. For the first time I heard that there were people called 'art therapists', and I resolved to become one. (Waller, 1987: 188)

In addition to the many informal presentations of patients work organised by Hill, Adamson and others, a number of public exhibitions were held during the 1950s and 1960s. In 1955, the Institute for Contemporary Art (ICA) in London hosted an exhibition entitled *Aspects of Schizophrenic Art*.[1] A decade later in 1964 the ICA organised another exhibition of art works made by psychiatric patients under the title *Art as Communication*. These and later exhibitions of 'psychiatric art' played an important role in drawing the public's attention to the individualistic and often highly expressive quality of the art work produced in psychiatric hospitals and to the contribution made by art therapists in this. The catalogue for one such exhibition, *The Inner Eye*, held at the Museum of Modern Art in Oxford in 1978, for example, contains a number of essays by prominent art therapists of that era; including Peter Byrne, Michael Edwards, John Henzell and Diana Halliday (Elliott, 1978).

Irene Champernowne and the Withymead Centre

Another important ingredient in the emergence of art therapy as a profession was the work carried out at the Withymead Centre in Devon. This therapeutic community pioneered the combined use of psychotherapy and the arts in the treatment of mental health problems (Stevens, 1986). Founded in 1942 by Irene and Gilbert Champernowne, the Withymead Centre provided a therapeutic environment distinctly different to that found in most mental hospitals at that time. It also served a very different clientele; primarily fee-paying patients drawn from the professional classes.

The Withymead Centre exercised a significant influence of the development of art therapy in the UK. As Waller states,

> It provided some of the first informal training schemes in the subject in the 1950s and 1960s. It was a source of personal learning and therapy for several founder members of the British Association of Art Therapists (many of whom later became prominent in teaching and research); and its founder, Irene Champernowne, actively campaigned for art therapy until her death, aged 75, in 1976. (1991: 61)

According to Hogan (2001: 256), both Hill and Adamson visited the centre, as did the psychiatrist R.D. Laing.

The therapeutic work conducted at the Withymead Centre was Jungian in orientation and placed the use of art as therapy at its heart. While in Zurich in the late 1930s Irene Champernowne had been in analysis with Carl Jung and his close colleague Toni Wolff. During her time in Zurich, Champernowne became familiar with Jung's theories and experienced for herself the value of image making as a means of self-exploration. Waller (1991) suggests that the experience of working simultaneously with two therapists was influential in the approach she later adopted at the Withymead Centre. This approach made a clear distinction between the work undertaken by the psychotherapist and the art therapist; 'The art therapist would help the patient to produce the pictures but it was the psychotherapist who would enter into the deeper meaning of the work' (Waller, 1991: 63). Viewed from this perspective, the role of the art therapist was like that of a midwife, to help facilitate a natural process in the service of rebirth and healing. Hogan (2001: 227) considers this assessment to be 'too simple and does not do justice to actual practices at Withymead'. These practices being, in Hogan's view, less rigid and more flexible than this dichotomy suggests.

Although the Withymead Centre closed in the late 1960s, its philosophy continues to be promoted through events organised by the Champernowne Trust.

Pioneering Art Therapy

Throughout the 1960s and 1970s, united by a conviction that painting and drawing provided a valuable creative outlet for individuals otherwise deprived of opportunities for self-expression and communication, an increasing number of artists and art teachers found employment in hospitals and clinics. These art therapists, often working in isolation from one another, developed differing ways of working and philosophies regarding the therapeutic potential of art. During this period, art therapists appear to have relied less on theory and more on intuition, respect for the image and warmth towards its maker in their approach. Describing the experience of taking over the art therapy department at Bowden Hill Clinic in Harrow-on-the-Hill from E.M Lyddiatt in the 1960s, Thomson recalls,

> It was a place that provoked dreams, a place where the 'introverted activity' of spontaneous imaginative work was safely housed … People could get the key to work in the art rooms whenever they wanted to. They were also free to come and go on the three mornings a week that the art therapist was present … I was amazed to see people she had spoken to in the main building come over and settle down to paint or model as though it was the most natural thing in the world. (1997: 16–17)

An Asylum Within an Asylum

The notion that the art therapy studio might function as an asylum within an asylum, a safe haven where freedom of expression was both permitted and encouraged, proved to be a popular and enduring one. The large institutions in which many art therapists were employed until they began to close in the 1980s and 1990s were more often than not overcrowded, impoverished, isolated, restrictive and extremely difficult institutions within which to conduct effective therapeutic work (Edwards, 1986, 1989). Many art therapists came to perceive their role as that of improving the quality of life of the people who lived in these hospitals. United by a shared belief in the power of images to embody and communicate needs, wishes and fears, art therapists sought to provide opportunities for self-fulfilment, self-understanding and self-healing. Art therapy was seen as a way of fostering self-esteem, promoting social interaction and self-expression, as well as beginning to address the sense of inner emptiness many patients experienced (Charlton, 1984; Molloy, 1997; Skailes, 1997; Wood, 1992). As Wood (2000: 45) comments, 'Those of us … who were working at the end of the 1970s spoke about the hospital art studio as being a refuge from the ravages of psychiatry'. Whether or not it was intended, art therapy often came to be perceived as a subversive activity, a form of therapy that stood in opposition to the values and assumptions embodied in mainstream psychiatry. During this period many art therapists allied themselves to, or were influenced by, the anti-psychiatry movement and humanistic forms of therapy.

Anti-Psychiatry

'Anti-psychiatry' is the term loosely applied to the critique of psychiatry and psychiatric practices provided by, among others, Thomas Szasz (1974, 1977) and R.D. Laing (1970, 1975). The social changes taking place in the Western world during the 1960s made a significant impact upon psychiatry, and upon the ways in which many art therapists thought about their work. As Henzell (1997b: 184) observes, the revolutionary politics of the 1960s proceeded in two directions, 'outwards towards social action and inwards towards psychological experience ... [especially] a consciousness which was to be 'raised', 'expanded', 'altered', 'changed', or 'in other ways transformed'. In a manner similar to that of the Romantic period, madness again became a matter of intellectual interest and public concern. Henceforth, the understanding and treatment of mental illness was seen as a human and social problem, rather than a purely medical one.

While there has been a tendency, as Wood (1991: 15) comments, to 'dismiss the effects of Laing's work as part of the heady psychedelic ramblings of a hippy culture', he was, through both his writing and personal charisma, able to challenge the de-humanising influence of mainstream psychiatry. As Wood also notes,

> Since Laing it is much more difficult for people to watch or read accounts of the process of psychiatric diagnosis in a way which can remain naïve about how culturally biased and how potentially harmful it is. (1991: 16).

The influence of the anti-psychiatry movement helped to foster a climate of rebelliousness and challenge within the emerging art therapy profession. Although the profession may have lost something of its radicalism in recent years, the enduring legacy of anti-psychiatry is most evident in the commitment many art therapists have to ensuring those individuals who would not ordinarily be considered suitable for counselling or psychotherapy have access to non-medical, psychotherapeutic sources of help.

Mary Barnes

An important link between art therapy and anti-psychiatry was the work of the artist Mary Barnes. Barnes became a psychiatric cause célèbre largely through her paintings, many of which were later exhibited throughout Britain and Europe. In 1963, after reading Laing's book *The Divided Self* (1970), Barnes became his patient. In 1965, Mary moved to Kingsley Hall, at Bromley-by-Bow in London, a therapeutic community set up by Laing and his colleagues as an alternative environment to that provided in psychiatric hospitals. From 1965 to 1970, she came under the care of Laing's colleague Joseph Berke and underwent regression therapy with him. It was during this time that she discovered her gift for painting. To begin with Barnes used her own excrement. Later, Berke offered her paper and crayons as an alternative way of expressing herself. The resulting images, which appeared to come screaming out of her psyche unadulterated by training or inhibition, were astounding. The most enduring image, to which she constantly returned, was that of the Crucifixion. In this she appeared to convey not only the agony of the cross but also the joy of the resurrection; a reflection, perhaps, of her own experience. The inspirational story of Mary's dramatic disintegration into infantile behaviour and her slow, painful reintegration as a creative adult, came to the public's attention, including that of many art therapists working at the time, through the book she later co-wrote with Joseph Berke, *Mary Barnes: Two Accounts Of A Journey Through Madness* (Berke and Barnes, 1973) and later still through David Edgar's play 'Mary Barnes', which was based on the book.

The Emergence of Art Therapy as a Profession

Due largely to the influence of the British Association of Art Therapists, formed in 1964, from the mid-1960s onwards art therapists increasingly began to assert their unique identity, emphasise their professionalism and to lobby for improved pay and conditions of employment. As Gilroy and Hanna (1998: 261) observe, art therapy during the 1960s and 1970s was characterised by an 'allegiance to the anti-psychiatry movement (and sometimes left-wing politics), plus an extreme resistance to being allied with occupational therapists, the medical model and the poorly paid paramedical professions'. This stance was not universally welcomed. As Thomson (1997: 57) remarks, '"Professionalism" ousted "woolliness" at some cost'. What I understand Thomson to mean by this is that art therapists, particularly those who had undertaken the kind of training then available, began to import into their work practices activities such as theme led groups she regards as antithetical to 'a truly creative experience' (Thomson, 1997: 57).

Art Therapy in the Public Sector

A preoccupying concern of art therapists in the UK from the 1960s onwards has been the establishment of a profession firmly rooted in the National Health Service, the training for which is also based in the public sector (Waller, 1991; see Chapter 6). This position is in marked contrast to that adopted by psychoanalysis and most other forms of verbal psychotherapy, where both practice and training remain largely based in the private sector. However, as there was no agreed definition of what art therapy was prior to 1982 when the Department of Health and Social Security published its Personnel Memorandum PM82/6, conflicts over identity and control of the profession began to surface during this period.[2] While differences between art therapy and other art based therapeutic activities such as those undertaken by art teachers or occupational therapists were increasingly emphasised, it also appears to have been the case that differences of approach within art therapy were largely played down. Commenting on the profession during this period, Waller (1987: 192) states,

It is probably true to say that most art therapists at that time saw art therapy as an 'alternative' treatment. Some were suspicious that colleagues might be tempted to 'sell out' and ascribe a 'medical' orientation to their work in the hope of easier recognition by the National Health Service. Others feared too 'educational' an approach, which might risk censor from the NHS. These anxieties, and the various differences of opinion which have to exist within a health organisation, were submerged during the intense campaign to achieve professional recognition.

It was not until the mid-1980s that disagreements within the profession in the UK regarding matters of theory and practice began to emerge.

Consolidation

The third and current phase of art therapy's development identified by Wood (1997) begins in the early 1980s. An era now principally remembered for its conservative politics and the promotion of individualism, deregulation and privatisation. Although the 1980s witnessed cutbacks in public expenditure, the decade was also a period of expansion and consolidation for art therapy. Increasing numbers of art therapists trained and joined the profession, and in 1982 a career and salary structure was established for art therapists working in the NHS. Though often taken for granted, it was extremely difficult for art therapists to convince those responsible for the provision of health care that individuals who initially trained as artists could play any role, let alone a significant one, in the treatment or rehabilitation of patients.

As the large psychiatric and 'mental handicap' hospitals contracted and eventually closed, art therapists were provided with new opportunities, as well as new challenges (Woddis, 1992). One important consequence of the move into community based or other specialised services, was that art therapists began to rethink the ways in which they had traditionally worked. As Wood (1997: 145) observes, during this period 'art therapists have lived through many changes in public sector legislation, the increasing professionalisation of their work and a more obvious linking of it to models from psychoanalysis, psychotherapy and group processes'.

The Growing Influence of Psychoanalysis

As art therapists in the UK began to draw more overtly upon psychoanalytic theory and practice in order to support their work, increasing importance came to be attached to the setting in which art therapy was practiced and to the relationship established between the art therapist and the client. Hogan (2001: 110 f/n), citing the work of Margaret Naumberg in particular, suggests that 'This shift within British art therapy may have been partly the consequence of publications arriving from the USA'. While the art therapy literature emanating from North America undoubtedly inspired and helped substantiate the work of art therapists in the UK, so too did the work of indigenous psychoanalysts like Donald Winnicott (1971) and Marion Milner (1969, 1971) who were sympathetic to the therapeutic potential inherent in image making. The distinguished art therapist Rita Simon, for example, drew inspiration from the ideas and insights found in Milner's influential book *On Not Being Able to Paint* (Milner, 1971). What appears to have first enthused Simon about Milner's work was her use of doodling as a means of liberating the imagination and her understanding of those underlying emotions that interfere with or inhibit this (Simon, 1988).

Nowadays, due principally to the nature of the training art therapists undertake, the influence of psychoanalysis is very marked within art therapy. The *Core Course Requirements for Postgraduate Art Therapy Training*, for example, explicitly states that, 'Art therapy is a form of psychotherapy and its training should be firmly rooted in psychotherapeutic concepts' (BAAT, 1992a). In this context the term 'psychotherapeutic' is understood to mean, 'the engagement in a therapeutic alliance between therapist and client and the interpersonal relationship that is central to this process' (BAAT, 1992a). As Case observes,

> The development of art therapy training to encompass psychodynamic modes of thinking and personal therapy reflects a necessity to work with other processes outside the picture as well as to deepen understanding within the picture making processes. (2000: 27)

Theories and methods of working derived from psychoanalysis have been incorporated into art therapy in a variety of ways. This is particularly evident in the way the relationship between the client and art therapist is structured and understood. The relationship between psychoanalysis and art as found in art therapy is examined in more detail in the following chapter.

Notes

1. The *Aspects of Schizophrenic Art* exhibition was curated by Professor G.M. Carstairs, who later became the first President of the British Association of Art Therapists (Waller, 1991: 103).

2. DHSS Personnel Memorandum PM82/6 provided the first 'official' definition of an art therapist as 'a person who is responsible for organising appropriate programmes of art activities of a therapeutic application with patients, individually or in groups, and possesses a degree in art or design or a qualification considered equivalent for entry to an accepted postgraduate training course, and also a qualification in art therapy following the completion of an accepted course at a recognised institution of further or higher education'.

4

FRAMES OF REFERENCE: PSYCHOANALYSIS, ART AND ART THERAPY

Art and the 'Inner World'

Human beings are, by nature, social. We need and depend upon relationships with others in order to survive and develop. The more cut off from human relations in the outer world a person becomes, the more likely they are to resort to emotionally charged fantasy. At its most extreme, a person might become so immersed or confined within their inner world that their relationship with the external world becomes tenuous or distorted beyond recognition. Clients seen in art therapy frequently complain of feeling disconnected or alienated from themselves or other people. At other times, they may feel overwhelmed or persecuted by them.

For many art therapists, the origins of these difficulties reside in past relationship problems. That is to say, in those desires, fears, losses and deprivations the client previously experienced in relation to significant people in their lives. Though opinions vary on the mechanisms and processes involved, it is believed that these past experiences, both good and bad, are internalised and incorporated into our 'inner world'.[1] Because these internalised experiences were often initially felt to be unpleasant, unacceptable or frightening they were banished (repressed) from consciousness, yet remain active and influential in the unconscious (Mollon, 2000). Theories concerning the unconscious mind vary considerably, but in psychotherapeutic work of the kind with which art therapists are involved the word 'unconscious' is usually used to refer to 'all those contents [of the mind] that are not present in the field of consciousness at a given moment' (Laplanche and Pontalis, 1988: 474). From this perspective, our inner worlds and our relationships with other people, are governed by feelings and mental processes the nature of which we are largely unaware.

In practice, art therapy is often concerned with gaining access to and making sense of this unknown or unacknowledged 'inner world' and the ways in which it influences relationships in the external world. The ways of working developed by art therapists are based largely upon the belief that through making images and objects, and the relationship between the art therapist and the client, long buried conflicts and feelings may find expression. By facilitating the emergence of inner experiences, within the secure environment provided by the art therapist, the client is offered an opportunity to further their self-understanding. Through externalising internal experience it becomes possible to stand apart from, think about and change it. Psychoanalysis has played such an important role in the development of art therapy largely because it offers both a method and body of ideas for accessing and understanding the unconscious mind. Of particular importance here has been the attention paid by psychoanalytic writers, from Freud onwards, to dreams and other forms of symbolising activity, including play and art (see Adams, 1993; Fuller, 1980; Glover, 2000; Kris, 1988). However, although psychoanalytic theory underpins much contemporary art therapy practice, its dominant influence has not been unchallenged.

Some Concerns About the Influence of Psychoanalysis on Art Therapy

Psychoanalysis has, without doubt, had a profound impact on twentieth-century thought and culture. Most of us are familiar with such terms as the 'Freudian slip' or the so-called 'Freudian symbol'. Many psychoanalytic ideas have found their way into culture through literature, cinema, advertising and art. The assimilation of psychoanalytic terms and concepts into everyday language has not, however, been accomplished without a degree of scepticism or resistance. Psychoanalysis has frequently been criticised for being obscure, out-dated, unscientific, preoccupied with sex or for paying insufficient attention to external reality. These alleged shortcomings are, to some extent, further compounded by the arcane, quasi-scientific language of psychoanalysis. Terms like 'object', 'ego', 'id', 'super-ego', 'libido', 'complex' and so on abound in the psychoanalytic literature (see Laplanche and Pontalis, 1988; Rycroft, 1979).

For some art therapists the reliance upon psychoanalytic theory has been at best limiting and at worst abusive. Hogan (1997: 38), arguing for a feminist art therapy, is particularly critical of art therapists who draw upon psychoanalytic theory in their work, believing that they 'are imposing ridiculous, arid, outdated and often misogynistic ideas about psychic development onto their patients'. For Hogan, it is vital that the art therapy process be capable of, 'Enabling women to understand, question and challenge the social and cultural conditions which are responsible for definition as "mad" or deviant' (1997: 38).

Silverstone (1997), whose approach to art therapy is based upon the theories of Carl Rogers, is no less critical in her assessment of the core beliefs held by art therapists whose theoretical frameworks and clinical practice are psychoanalytic in orientation. To work with images in a person-centred way entails, according to Silverstone, the strict avoidance of anything that might be defined as the 'interpretation' of a client's image. To do so is perceived as hindering the personal development of the client. In Silverstone's view, 'Person-centeredness aims to empower the person; interpreting does the opposite. This is the central difference between person-centred art therapy and other, more psychodynamic approaches' (1997: 268). This assessment of psychoanalytically informed art therapy is based on the view that art therapists who are not person-centred in their approach might be perceived as the expert who knows best what an image means and that this fosters a sense of dependence rather than autonomy. Mindful of such criticisms, particularly in relation to issues of 'difference' concerning race, ethnicity, class, gender or sexual orientation, art therapists seek to address this imbalance of power in their work; (see Campbell et al., 1999; Hiscox and Calisch, 1998; Hogan, 1997).

Psychoanalysis and Art Therapy

For all its alleged or actual failings, the influence of psychoanalysis on art therapy as it is currently practiced in the UK and elsewhere in the world has been extensive. In order to further their understandings of the 'inner world' and its imaginative products art therapists have drawn extensively upon psychoanalytic theory, albeit in different ways. Theories and concepts derived from psychoanalysis have been incorporated into art therapy in three main ways:

- The first of these concerns the way psychoanalytic theory and practices have influenced the structure and organisation of art therapy. This includes establishing and maintaining appropriate therapeutic boundaries.
- Secondly, psychoanalytic theories have been enormously influential in informing the ways in which the therapeutic process is understood. Especially important here are psychoanalytic theories concerning defence mechanisms, play, transference and countertransference phenomena.
- Finally, and possibly most controversially, psychoanalysis has undoubtedly had an effect on the way images clients make in art therapy are interpreted.

In the remainder of this chapter I shall explore some of the ways in which ideas drawn from psychoanalysis have shaped the clinical practice of art therapy.

Boundaries and Frames

Boundaries define a space set aside for a particular purpose. Many spaces (the sports arena, temple, stage, court of justice, etc.) have this function and within them special rules apply; 'All are temporary worlds within the ordinary world, dedicated to the performance of an act apart' (Huizinga, 1949: 10). The art room or studio is also a space dedicated to a particular purpose and the boundaries which encompass this space are similarly intended to allow for the creation of temporary, symbolic worlds. In art therapy, the edges of a sheet of paper or the frame surrounding a painting also help us distinguish between the realm of the imagination and everyday reality. Boundaries are particularly important in art therapy because without them it would not be possible to differentiate between the literal and the symbolic or between internal and external reality.

It was the psychoanalyst Marion Milner who first used the metaphor of the picture frame when discussing the importance of providing boundaries for the analytic situation (Milner, 1952). Through exploring the links between the framed experience of the therapy situation and that of the art gallery and artist's studio, Schaverien (1989, 1992) extends the metaphor of the frame, using it to distinguish art therapy from other forms of therapy in which art is employed. In her discussion of this issue, Schaverien attaches particular importance to art therapists' own experiences of image making and to the picture within the frame, 'The picture within the frame is the space where transferences may be illustrated, revealed and enacted ... The picture, safely contained within the boundaries of the edges of the paper, reveals the imaginal world' (1992: 77).

There are many elements to the therapeutic frame, including the frequency and duration of sessions, in addition to the length and type of therapy on offer (A. Gray, 1994). As a physical space, it consists of a room or studio that is quiet, comfortable, appropriately equipped and free from interruption. As far as possible, the therapy space should remain constant and familiar. In many situations, however, art therapists often experience considerable difficulty establishing and maintaining these boundaries. As Molloy (1997: 251) comments, 'If these elementary criteria are not met, psychotherapeutic work becomes extremely difficult if not impossible'.

The boundaries of the therapeutic space are also indicated by a set of conventions concerning how both the art therapist and client should conduct themselves. For the client, this may entail agreeing to start and finish sessions on time and that all images and objects made in art therapy sessions remain in the art room until therapy has ended. The art therapist's behaviour will be guided by the principles of professional practice and codes of ethics to which they subscribe. This includes maintaining the therapist–client relationship on a professional basis at all times (BAAT, 1994). Unfortunately, boundary violations are not uncommon in art therapy. Examples include client's arriving late, missing sessions or, in private practice, not paying fees on the agreed date. Art therapists may break the boundaries of the therapeutic relationship by extending the length of a session or disclosing personal information about themselves. In each case, such boundary violations may be regarded as significant. This kind of activity, where thinking is replaced by action, is referred to in the psychoanalytic literature as 'acting out' (Rycroft, 1979: 1).

The purpose of the therapeutic frame is to provide safety and minimise uncertainty (Young, 1998). This is essential for psychotherapeutic work to occur. Without the security provided by the therapeutic frame clients would be unable to share those thoughts, feelings and experiences that are too shameful or distressing to express or communicate elsewhere. The essence of the therapeutic frame is that it provides a physical and mental space where feelings can be held in order to facilitate creativity and emotional growth. Setting limits enables anxiety to be contained. The concept of containment has been of particular importance to art therapists working with very damaged or regressed clients.

Containment

The term 'containment' has its origins in the writings of the psychoanalyst Wilfred Bion (1967). The concept refers to an inner space filled with feelings and thoughts, which are projected out from or internalised into the space of the container (see Hinshelwood, 1991). From very early in life we are intimately aware of our bodies as containers into which we put things and out of which other things materialise. We also experience the physical environment as something by which we are surrounded and from which we can emerge. We move in and out of rooms, clothes, relationships, jobs and other kinds of bounded spaces. Many of the metaphors found in everyday speech are based on this concept. One can be 'self-contained' or 'out of one's mind'. In art therapy, the art therapist, studio and available art materials may also assume this containing function (see Greenwood, 1994; Killick, 2000). Just as a parent might be said to accept, contain and survive the distressed infants fears, and to return these in a modified, less toxic form, the therapeutic relationship may help the client through a similar process of transformation.

> Once the child or client has a sense of someone [or something] with this containing function within, the capacity for thought and for tolerating bad feelings is increased ... The ability to hold and contain sense without simply evacuating it into someone else has then been taken in. A sense of space and time is created; experience does not have to be rejected or incorporated immediately but can be held for a while. Thoughts and thinking become possible. (J. Segal, 1992: 122)

Though part and parcel of therapeutic work, containing and thinking about feelings the client experiences as unbearable may be extremely demanding for the art therapist. During a session the art therapist may, for example, feel drained, attacked or filled with feelings of helplessness or despair.

'Sue'

For Sue, the need for containment, and the difficulties associated with acting out, were central themes in our work together. At times she would flood the sessions with material; either by producing large amounts of quickly and often messily executed artwork or talking for long periods without interruption. In either case, she demanded I gave what she was doing my full attention. If I appeared to be failing to do this, or if I misunderstood the meaning of her images and words, Sue would become extremely upset and angry. Sue would often express her anger by destroying the image she was working on or, contrary to our agreement, take her pictures away with her at the end of the session. At times it was as if Sue wished to fill all the available space and, wherever possible, extend this as far as possible. As this behaviour increased, maintaining the therapeutic frame became increasingly difficult.

At the beginning of one particularly memorable session, Sue emptied the contents of the carrier bag she had arrived with on to the floor. She then proceeded to scatter these torn and discarded images and pieces of writing around the room, all the time complaining bitterly that they were rubbish and that I thought she was rubbish. She then curled up in a corner of the room and began quietly sobbing. In response, I sat near her, letting her know I was nearby but saying nothing further, having learnt from previous similar encounters that she found this intrusive and overwhelming. As her crying and fury subsided Sue began to describe how she had felt at the end of our previous session and over the course of the following week. She felt my failure to understand her was a rejection. More than this, she felt I could never understand her, but that even if I did I would reject her anyway.

This ambivalence about emotional intimacy lay at the very heart of Sue's interpersonal difficulties, although it was only much later in our work together that the internal conflicts contributing to this dynamic became apparent and could be openly explored in the art therapy sessions. Sue felt I wanted to get rid of her, and seemed to be relating to me in such a way as to provoke just such a response. The emotional climate of the sessions at this time oscillated between impingement and abandonment. If I was perceived as being too close, or too far away, Sue would become increasingly anxious. If I asked her about her

4.1   Sue

images, she felt I was trying to get inside her mind. If I remained silent, I was experienced as hostile and uncaring. Underlying these exchanges were almost palpable, but otherwise unexpressed, feelings of frustration, rage, fear and despair.

Sue craved the security afforded by a safe, containing relationship, but at the same time feared it. In particular she feared the consequences of allowing anyone access to her inner world. To do so was to risk losing her sense of self through being controlled by someone else, a fear that had its origins in early infancy. Through turning her artwork and art therapy into rubbish Sue was able to protect herself from these feelings, albeit only temporarily. Though effective,

this stratagem also left Sue feeling empty and uncontained.[2]
Tempting though it often was, I did not reject Sue through prema-
turely ending our work together. But it was only after many months
of struggling to contain and think about the meaning of Sue's acting
out behaviour that she felt sufficiently able to trust the integrity of
the frame to begin to make productive use of the therapeutic possi-
bilities it offered.

Inhibition

While many clients seen in art therapy have little difficulty making
images, for some doing so can be both frightening and inhibiting. It is for
this reason that the feelings experienced by the client when faced with a
blank sheet of paper are just as important as those associated with the
finished picture. There may be numerous reasons why an individual finds
it difficult to engage with either the available materials or the art therapist.
Often this is because the client is afraid to change. For some clients,
image making may be perceived as a harmful self-indulgence, whereas for
others their fear is rooted in the belief that the inner world contains forces
so dangerous or destructive that if given expression they may cause dis-
aster or provoke revenge. Other fears and anxieties touched upon in art
therapy include the fear of losing control, an over-dependence on the
views and approval of others and the dread of ridicule or humiliation
(Gordon, 1983).

The reticence to fully engage with art therapy may be articulated
through such comments as 'I can't draw', 'Painting is childish', or 'I've
never been any good at art and I'm too old to change now'. Wood (1986)
suggests that one way of addressing the anxiety associated with beginning art therapy is to invite the client to remember how they drew and
painted when they were children, the aim being to help allay the clients'
fear that they are expected to make Art. Other art therapists may attempt
to overcome these fears by suggesting a theme or employing 'warm-up'
exercises (see Leibmann, 1999). If the understandable fears clients have
about making images are not acknowledged, understood and responded
to with sensitivity the client may simply leave. Alternatively, they may feel
obliged to participate, but will do so without any emotional involvement,
producing images that are formulaic or stereotyped. It is a mistake to
assume that because a client may draw or paint they are necessarily
engaged with the creative process. To give a feeling form and produce an
image that is in some way meaningful and personally significant involves
the risk of abandoning the familiar and courting the unknown. This can
feel messy, chaotic, terrifying. Mann (1990a) suggests that the use of art
in therapy might not only be non-creative, it may also be anti-creative. That

is to say, image making may be employed defensively in order to avoid emotional pain.

On Not Being Able to Paint

One of the most influential psychoanalytic perspectives on creative inhibition is that offered by Marion Milner in her book *On Not Being Able to Paint* (Milner, 1971). Milner wrote this book after she began making free association or 'doodle' drawings during the first years of her own analysis. For Milner, the anxiety that inhibits a person's ability to paint is often based in the fear of the loss of a sense of self. A fear originating, Milner suggests, in an inability to trust the capacity of the imagination to transform the raw material of the unconscious into art. Through her own struggle to make images, Milner came to better understand the importance of abandoning self-consciousness and of blurring the boundary between 'me' and 'not-me' in order to create something original and meaningful. By allowing hand and eye to do exactly what pleased them, without any conscious working to a preconceived intention, Milner discovered she was capable of producing drawings entirely different from those she had been taught or, indeed, expected to make. As Milner puts it, 'it was only when I had discarded this wish to copy that the resulting drawing or painting had any life in it, any of the sense of a living integrated structure existing in its own right' (Milner, 1971: 154).

Anxiety and Defence Mechanisms

The psychological defences we employ to protect ourselves from feeling anxious or distressed are both significant and necessary. These defence mechanisms seek to protect us from being consciously aware of thoughts and feelings we cannot tolerate. They operate by only allowing unconscious thoughts or feelings to be expressed indirectly, often in a disguised form. Some of the more familiar defence mechanisms include:

- *Denial*: Where a thought of feeling is rejected outright, e.g. 'Of course I don't miss him/her!'
- *Projection*: Where a feeling is disowned and attributed to someone or something else, e.g. 'I don't hate him/her, they hate me!'
- *Rationalisation*: This defence works through offering an explanation intended to justify a belief or point of view while also denying a feeling; e.g. 'I'm not upset by the way X treats me, he/she are under a lot of pressure at work.'

All defence mechanisms serve the purpose of reducing anxiety. Some defence mechanisms, however, may be thought of as being more mature or constructive than others. This is particularly true of sublimation.

Sublimation

What distinguishes sublimation from other defence mechanisms is its social value. As noted in Chapter 2, 'sublimation' was the term Freud introduced into the psychoanalytic literature to account for the process by which unacceptable impulses are re-shaped in the service of psychological and cultural development. As Rycroft (1979: 159) notes, 'All sublimations depend on symbolization and all ego-development depends on sublimation'. It is through the process of sublimation that sexual or aggressive feelings are transformed into socially valuable or productive forms such as artistic creation or intellectual enquiry. Without this capacity, Freud argued, there could be no such thing as civilisation (Freud, 1991).

It is the American art therapist Edith Kramer who has most explicitly championed the value and relevance of this concept to art therapy. For Kramer, sublimation lies at the very heart of her belief in the healing potential of art. It is through the process of sublimation, she argues, that primitive asocial impulses may be transformed into socially productive acts, 'so that the pleasure in the achievement of the social act replaces the pleasure which gratification of the original urge would have afforded' (Kramer, 2000: 41). It is necessary to draw a distinction here between sublimation and substitution. In the latter, one thing is replaced with another; as, for example, when we might thump a pillow rather than a person. Sublimation, by contrast, involves a process of change. That is to say, through drawing or painting feelings of frustration or anger may be transformed into something more constructive. In Kramer's view, the art therapist's primary function is to, 'Assist the process of sublimation, an act of integration and synthesis which is performed by the ego, wherein the peculiar fusion between reality and fantasy, between the unconscious and the conscious, which we call art is reached' (Kramer in Ulman, 2001: 19).

It follows from this that there is a direct correlation between the quality of an artwork and the degree of sublimation involved in its creation. In effect, the more accomplished and aesthetically pleasing the artwork, the more complete the sublimation might be said to be. In practice this approach to art therapy involves encouraging the client to achieve the highest possible level of creative attainment they are capable of. This way of working stands in marked contrast to that adopted by those art therapists who favour the production of spontaneous, quickly executed images as a means of facilitating cathartic expression or further, verbal, exploration.

For Kramer, the evidence of the depth and strength of the process of sublimation is to be found in an artwork's 'evocative power, inner consistency, and economy of artistic means … the harmony of art is attained through the integration and balance of tensions' (Kramer in Junge and Asawa, 1994: 36). The emphasis Kramer places on the relationship between form and content in art therapy is similar to that advocated by Maclagan (2001) and Schaverien (2000). The approach to art therapy developed by both these UK based art therapists is, however, rooted in the Jungian tradition of working with images rather than the psychoanalytic one.

Playing and Reality

As previously noted, Freud considered imaginative activities such as dreaming, fantasising (daydreaming), playing and the creation of art as means of accumulating pleasure by re-arranging reality into new and more congenial forms. The connection Freud makes between creativity and play is discussed in his 1908 paper 'Creative Writers and day-dreaming'. He writes,

> Might we not say that every child at play behaves like a creative writer, in that he creates a world of his own, or, rather, re-arranges the things of his world in a new way which pleases him? ... The creative writer does the same as the child at play. He creates a world of phantasy which he takes very seriously – that is, which he invests with large amounts of emotion – while separating it sharply from reality. (Freud, 1975, vol. IX: 144)

In Freud's view, the essential characteristic of play, indeed all forms of imaginative activity, was its unreality. For Freud, the unreality of imaginative activity is of crucial importance. Without it, that which is represented, were it real, could give no enjoyment, neither could that which is distressing become a source of pleasure.

It was also Freud's belief that in growing up the individual is obliged to stop playing and face the realities of life. Freud recognised, however, that a total renunciation of the pleasures experienced through play is impossible.

> Whoever understands the human mind knows that hardly anything is harder for a man than to give up a pleasure which he has once experienced. Actually, we can never give anything up; we only exchange one thing for another. (Freud, 1975, vol. IX: 145)

From this perspective, fantasising is what adult's do instead of playing, although with one significant difference. Whereas, in Freud's assessment, a child makes no attempt to conceal his play, he contends that the adult 'is ashamed of his phantasies and hides them from other people' (Freud, 1975, vol. IX: 145). In asserting the view that play and other forms of imaginative activity were essentially ways of avoiding reality and therefore symptomatic of neurosis Freud neglects their positive and adaptive nature. The psychoanalyst D.W. Winnicott challenged this view, arguing that playing involves a creative encounter with reality resulting in real and beneficial changes to both the internal and external world. Commenting on this issue in relation to Freud's concept of sublimation, Winnicott states,

> Freud did not have a place in his topography of the mind for the experience of things cultural... Freud used the word 'sublimation' to point the way to a place where cultural experience is meaningful, but perhaps he did not get so far as to tell us where in the mind cultural experience is. (1980: 112)

For Winnicott, the place where cultural experience is located is in the 'potential space between the individual and the environment ... Cultural experience begins with creative living first manifested in play' (Winnicott, 1980: 118). Winnicott suggests that the connection between internal and external reality, and between the self and others, is established through the use of what he terms 'transitional phenomena'. These phenomena or objects (teddy bear, blanket, etc.) are experienced as part of self *and* as part of the external world. A well-known example is Linus' 'security blanket' in Schultz's cartoon strip 'Peanuts'. 'It is true' Winnicott (1980: 6) states, 'that the piece of blanket (or whatever it is) is symbolical of some part-object, such as the breast. Nevertheless, the point of it is not its symbolic value so much as its actuality'. The fact that such transitional objects are not the breast or the mother is as important as the fact that they may symbolically represent them. This is because, 'When symbolism is employed the infant is already clearly distinguishing between fantasy and fact, between inner objects and external objects, between primary creativity and perception (Winnicott, 1980: 6). The function of transitional phenomena – which exist in the 'potential space' between objectivity and subjectivity – is to help children 'make the transition from infantile narcissism to object-love and from dependence to self-reliance' (Rycroft, 1979: 102). It was through the use of these objects, Winnicott argued, that the developing infant found his or her way into the worlds of play, creativity, symbolism and culture.

The 'Squiggle Game'

Winnicott regarded psychoanalysis as a specialised form of playing. Playing, he suggests, 'facilitates growth and therefore health; playing leads into group relationships; playing can be a form of communication in psychotherapy' (Winnicott, 1980: 48). A practical example of Winnicott's approach was the technique he employed in his therapeutic consultations with children. Winnicott called this the 'squiggle game' (Winnicott, 1971). In the spirit of playful communication, this simple game involved Winnicott drawing a few fairly random, neutral lines ('squiggles') on a sheet of paper and then passing this to the child to make into a picture. In turn, the child would start a drawing that Winnicott then completed. As the game went on, a visual and verbal dialogue would emerge facilitating communication between Winnicott and his young patients. Through these drawings, and the conversation around them, the child was able to express thoughts and feelings that had initially been impossible to put into words. Although Winnicott employed the squiggle game in order to get into contact with the child's unconscious, interpretation was not the main feature. His primary concern was to understand as comprehensively as possible the difficulties of the children he saw. In the introduction to his book, *Therapeutic Consultations in Child Psychiatry*, in which his use of the squiggle game is discussed, Winnicott writes,

Dogmatic interpretation leaves the child with only two alternatives, an acceptance of what I have said as propaganda or a rejection of the interpretation and of me and of the whole set-up. I think and hope that children in this relationship with me feel that they have the right to reject what I say or the way I take something. (1971: 10)

In other words, while the drawings that emerged in his therapeutic consultations were often suggestive of hidden conflicts, Winnicott was careful not to inhibit the child's ability to convey a sense of self through misinterpretation. Following Winnicott, art therapists endeavour to remain sensitive to this approach and to his observation that therapy,

Is done in the overlap between the two play areas, that of the patient and that of the therapist. If the therapist cannot play, then he is not suitable for the work. If the patient cannot play, then something needs to be done to enable the patient to become able to play, after which psychotherapy may begin. (Winnicott, 1980: 63)

For Winnicott, the capacity to play is essential to the therapeutic process because,

It is in playing and only in playing that the individual child or adult is able to be creative and to use the whole personality, and it is only in being creative that the individual discovers the self. (1980: 63)

In effect, self-discovery and self-understanding are grounded in the capacity to play.

Transference

The term 'transference' is used to denote 'the process by which a patient displaces on to the therapist attitudes adopted towards previous figures in the patient's life' (Lomas, 1994: 43). In effect, this transference is based on the unconscious assumption that feelings, attitudes and other characteristics derived from previous figures in our lives are possessed by the person to whom we are now relating. Although the unconscious repetition of an earlier relationship might occur in any relationship, it has particular meaning and significance within the boundaries of the therapeutic setting. Within psychoanalysis, 'the transference is acknowledged to be the terrain on which all the basic problems of a given analysis play themselves out: the establishment, modalities, interpretation and resolution of the transference are in fact what define the cure' (Laplanche and Pontalis, 1988: 455). This is not so for art therapy. While most art therapists now acknowledge its ubiquity, working with the transference is not necessarily a central aspect of their clinical practice (see Agell et al., 1981). For some art therapists 'the idea that today's relationships are shaped and haunted by yesterday's relationships with absent others merely introduces unnecessary complications' (Ulman in Agell et al., 1981: 5). And yet clients do relate towards art therapists in a variety of ways, ranging from denigration to idealisation, that suggest this is based more on how they imagine them to be, rather than how they actually are.

'Paula'

Paula began seeing me after an attempted suicide. Having initially been somewhat idealised by Paula, and seen by her as offering the solution to all her problems, as therapy progressed she became increasingly defensive and uncooperative. Long silences began to punctuate the art therapy sessions, and if she made images she often refused to say anything about them. When Paula did speak she described the world, and the people she met in it, almost exclusively in terms of feeling persecuted or attacked. It was also evident that she was experiencing similar feelings in relation to me.

As Paula's story began, slowly, to unfold, it became increasingly clear that in her relationship with me she was re-enacting feelings previously experienced in her relationship with her mother. She was also repeating many of the ways she had earlier developed in order to cope with these feelings. To begin with this had involved being on her best behaviour by being a 'good' client. Later, as her fear and anger intensified, she attempted to make herself as inaccessible and invisible as possible. Once Paula and I were able to see and understand her behaviour as a repetition of an earlier relationship her anxiety and defensiveness were substantially diminished.

Cantle makes the following observation with respect to the importance of understanding and working with the transference,

> The transference lets us know about that part of the client that cannot be borne by himself at the time and which seeks refuge within us until it is safe to incorporate it back in a less persecutory way. (1983: 9)

These unconscious communications can, and sometimes do, wound the art therapist, particularly when we are left with the feeling of having been rebuked, as of old, by a disapproving parent.

Countertransference

Countertransference may be understood as referring to the therapist's (unconscious) feelings towards the client. Laplanche and Pontalis (1988: 92) define countertransference as, 'The whole of the analyst's unconscious reactions to the individual analysand – especially to the analysand's own transference'. In practice there are two aspects to this. The first of these applies to the inappropriate or disproportionate feelings activated in the therapist as a consequence of his or her own life experiences. The art therapist may, for example, come to feel envious or hostile towards the client in much the same way they previously felt towards a parent or sibling. If the art therapist acted upon such feelings this would clearly prove damaging to the client. It is for this reason that art therapists are now required to gain an understanding of their own unconscious processes during training, and are expected to receive regular clinical supervision afterwards.

The second sense in which the word countertransference is used is when it is applied to describe the ways in which therapists make use of the feelings evoked in them as a means of understanding the client's inner world. In this sense, the therapist's countertransference is not a distorted perception, but an accurate one. In response to the client's transference, the art therapist may, for instance, come to feel distinctly maternal or paternal towards them (Mann, 1988). Through reflecting on these feelings the art therapist can arrive at a better understanding of the way the client is relating to them; that is, *as if* the therapist were indeed the client's parent. These two forms of countertransference might usefully be distinguished as 'active' and 'reactive' (Cairns, 1994: 304). The former referring to feelings activated within the therapist to counteract those of the client, the latter being responsive to the feelings of the client. Needless to say, distinguishing between the two is by no means easy and represents one of the greatest challenges art therapists face in their day-to-day practice.

Transference and Countertransference in Art Therapy

As noted above, not all art therapists work with transference and countertransference phenomena. This is usually because they regard image making as inherently therapeutic or because they view transference and countertransference phenomena as intruding upon or disrupting the creative process (Betensky, 1995; Kramer, 2000; Simon, 1992; Thomson, 1997). For many of these art therapists, working with the art in art therapy is of primary importance and central to their professional identity. Many other art therapists, while also regarding image making as central to their practice, have incorporated working with the transference and countertransference into their work (Case, 1996; McMurray and Schwartz, 1998; Mann, 1988; Naumberg, 1966). Differences of opinion on this issue have played a significant role in the title debate discussed in Chapter 1. Dalley, for example, unequivocally asserts,

> Whatever is decided about our professional title, it is my view that it is the art work and images with which we work and the understanding of transference and countertransference processes within the clear boundaries of the sessions that form the foundations of art therapy identity and practice. (2000: 87)

In the UK, Joy Schaverien has made a particularly significant contribution to debates within the profession regarding the effects of transference and countertransference in art therapy (see Schaverien, 1982, 1987, 1992, 1995,

2000). In seeking to reconcile the view that making art is intrinsically healing, while also acknowledging the therapeutic significance of the transference and countertransference, Schaverien argues that 'there are times when the picture, too, becomes an object of transference' (1995: 123). Drawing upon a range of psychological, anthropological and philosophical theories, but especially those of Jung and the philosopher Ernst Cassirer, Schaverien identifies two main ways by which materials and objects come to embody, through the transference, aspects of the inner world of the client. These she identifies as the scapegoat and the talisman (Schaverien, 1987, 1992). In both instances, images become emotionally invested and thus empowered. Schaverien also identifies two distinctly different kinds of pictures produced by clients in relation to this. These are the diagrammatic and embodied image; the difference 'reflects the transference that is made to the art work in the process of creation' (Schaverien, 2000: 59).

Diagrammatic and Embodied Images

Diagrammatic pictures are ones that, like the hurriedly drawn sketch, are not intrinsically significant, though they may reveal something of the client's inner world through depicting previously unconscious or unacknowledged feelings. Such pictures, however, usually lack emotional power. They tend to be descriptive of feelings rather than invested with feeling. The picture is an illustration of a feeling, rather than an embodiment of feeling in much the same way that a client might talk about feeling angry or sad without actually being in touch with these feelings. In contrast to the diagrammatic picture, with the embodied image,

> It is as if the picture-making process 'takes over'. No matter what the original intention, an image may be suggested by a line drawn a certain way, and an accidental splash or mark may be incorporated. Provided that the original intention is not too rigidly adhered to or fixed, the whole has a life, an evolution of its own. (Schaverien, 1987: 78)

Once an emotional investment has been made in the image, the pictures become alive and invested with feeling and meaning and through the image making process it becomes possible for the client to fully engage with their inner world.

> Images which were fused, locked in, appear outside on the paper, evidence to the client that she has these feelings, which then become inescapable but separate. It is at this point, at the point of recognition of the feeling, that the aesthetic quality of the images frequently changes, and develops. The pictures start to exhibit opposing elements and conflicts. Emotions which were repressed, which felt too difficult, too painful to face, become accessible, contained as they are 'out there' in the image, within the frame of the picture. (Schaverien, 1987: 78–79)

In practice, the distinction between diagrammatic and embodied images is not always as clear as Schaverien's schema suggests. Neither is it necessarily the case that diagrammatic images are without therapeutic value. They may be a necessary precursor for later and more emotionally invested images. They may also indicate that the client is in some way stuck or not yet ready to allow more personal feelings to surface in their image making.

'Mike'

The first images Mike produced in art therapy depicted his circumstances, as he perceived these at the time. He saw himself as hurtling at some speed towards the brick wall that stood between himself and the outside world. Beyond the wall and slightly ajar door, lay the wished for state of peace, calmness and tranquillity.

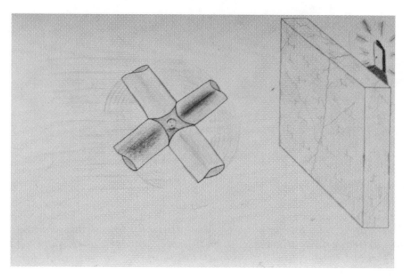

4.2 Mike

Following Schaverien's schema, this image might be said to illustrate his wish to feel different rather than expressing how he actually felt. When talking about this image, and the similar images that preceded it, Mike was insistent that if only he could force his way through to the other side of his problems he would be OK. What he didn't want to do was look at his problems or the obstacles that stood in his way.

As our work together continued, Mike gradually began to recognise that he could not simply smash his way through the difficulties that stood in his path. Indeed his previous attempts to do so, which included driving dangerously and getting into fights, served only to exacerbate his problems. As Mike began to face his problems, particularly his underlying feelings of anger and frustration, his artwork began to change, becoming more personal and invested with feeling. The first indication of this change was that Mike's images became messy as he began to allow himself more freedom to experiment with the art materials.

4.3 Mike

Fearing he was losing control, Mike initially found this change in his artwork quite distressing. With time, however, he discovered he was able to develop a personal language of shapes and forms. Through this developing visual language Mike was able to represent and begin to explore his feelings about his family and about himself.

The feelings invested in images made in art therapy can, and often do, have a distinct emotional impact upon both the client and the art therapist. Schaverien (1995) employs the term 'aesthetic countertransference' to describe the power of pictures to disturb or seduce (see also Case, 1996).

Although they have been challenged, most notably by Mann (1989; 1990b) Schaverien's ideas have nevertheless been widely adopted by art therapists currently working in the UK.

4.4   Mike

Understanding and Interpreting Images

The ability to create symbols provides the basis for all forms of human communication. As Hinshelwood (1991: 447) observes, 'The capacity to live in a world of symbols remote from the world of physical and biological objects is the hallmark of human development'. The means by which an individual is able to use objects and materials symbolically in order to represent, communicate or express thoughts, feelings and experiences is a matter of crucial importance in both psychoanalysis and art therapy. However, unlike psychoanalysis, which is essentially a verbal practice, art therapy is based upon the belief that states of mind that are beyond words may find expression through images in a symbolic form. In art therapy, two forms of symbolising activity are particularly relevant, the use of metaphor and symbol formation.

Metaphor

A metaphor is a figure of speech used to imply that the properties or qualities possessed by one thing are like those belonging to something else. A metaphor may be distinguished from a simile in that with the former the comparison between one thing and another is only implied, whereas in a simile it is explicitly stated through the use of words such as 'like' or 'as'. Visual metaphors function in much the same way as verbal metaphors and use imagery to evoke an idea or emotion beyond the specific object depicted.[3] We

61

may think of a line as 'nervous' or 'agitated', a shape as being 'bold' or a colour as 'shocking'. Metaphors are particularly useful in enabling us to express that which might otherwise be inexpressible. When we say we feel 'buried under a mountain of work' or are about to 'boil over' we are using a metaphor. Metaphors are an integral part of our daily lives and are present in everyday speech. Metaphor affects the way we think and feel, and how we express or communicate our thoughts and feelings to others (Lakoff and Johnson, 1980). Metaphorical thinking is so pervasive that we are often barely conscious of its influence.

Psychoanalytic theory is saturated with metaphors. Freud frequently used metaphor to both formulate and exemplify his ideas. An example of this is Freud's conception of the mind as a 'psychical apparatus'. That is, as a kind of 'engine' or 'machine' around which mental 'energy' might 'flow' or become 'dammed' (Freud, 1980). Since Freud, different psychoanalytic schools have introduced alternative metaphors to describe the ways the mind works, many of which have been incorporated into the language of art therapy. Salzberger-Wittenberg (1991: 27), for example, draws attention to the ways in which we use metaphor to describe psychological processes in terms of bodily, and especially digestive, functions; 'We speak of "taking in" knowledge and good experience, of "distasteful" ideas, of "digesting" facts, of "pouring out" our troubles, of "pushing" unwanted thoughts out of our mind as if they were physical entities'. It is through such metaphors that we are able to express our phantasies about what we contain and how emotional experiences may be internalised or expelled.[4] Thus, 'The elated person may feel full of knowledge, full of good experiences, full of love, and the depressed person may feel empty and full of rubbish' (Salzberger-Wittenberg, 1991: 27).

In art therapy clients frequently draw or paint metaphorically to express or evoke a mood or feeling. A picture of an isolated tree might, for instance, suggest a feeling of loneliness or despair, an erupting volcano, anger. If the client is unable to use images in this way, some art therapists may use visual exercises such as encouraging them to imagine themselves as an animal or an inanimate object and to represent themselves as such in a drawing or painting (see Liebmann, 1999). When metaphors emerge in art therapy, either in the client's conversation or through their image making, the art therapist's attention is alerted to the ways in which they reveal and possibly limit the client's thinking. Henzell (1984) draws a helpful distinction between 'framed' and 'unframed' metaphors in relation to this.

A framed metaphor is open to inspection, indeed it might be said to invite it; its frame prefaces with 'as if'. An 'unframed' metaphor is closed … the particular way an action is expressive, the figurative allusions involved, remain covert and unconscious, or unassimilated to conscious examination and criticism. (1984: 25)

Through becoming aware of the ways in which 'unframed' or 'dead' metaphors shape thoughts and feelings, and through creating new, 'framed' or 'live' metaphors, the client in art therapy may be able to transcend the literal.[5] To see that they are not actually about to 'explode', but are in fact 'agitated', 'wound up', 'fuming' or just plain angry. By changing the way we see things we might also begin to change the way we understand and feel about them.

Symbols

Symbols function in a similar way to metaphors. Symbols also represent one thing, such as an object, idea or feeling, by linking it with something else. Like a metaphor, a symbol stands for something beyond itself. Unlike metaphors, however, symbols usually have more than one meaning. Indeed it is the imprecise nature of symbols that provides the source for much of their emotive power. Moreover, symbols acquire significance through repetition, whereas the opposite is true for metaphors. The symbolic meaning of the images made by clients in art therapy is not always apparent and can take time to unravel. It is vitally important, therefore, that the art therapist is able to tolerate uncertainty and avoid jumping to a premature conclusion regarding what an image might mean. There are a number of reasons for this.

- Firstly, symbols acquire their meaning depending on the context in which they are created and used. A drawing of a house may be understood as the literal rendering of a place or, possibly, as a symbol of the self. The fact that clients may use the same symbol to express very different feelings further complicates the issue of understanding the meaning an image made in art therapy may have.
- Secondly, symbols may be private, public or a combination of the two. In works by Picasso, for instance, the bull functions as both a symbol of his nationality (through reference to the traditions of Spanish culture) and as a symbol of the artist himself; particularly his sense of masculinity (Berger, 1965). In art therapy, clients may also depict objects or use materials and colours in a manner that combines both public and private symbol systems. The colour red, for example, may be used symbolically to represent passion, danger or anger, in addition to more personal feelings and associations.
- Finally, because symbols posses this inherently ambivalent, either/or quality, the meaning of an image may be explicit or hidden, conscious or unconscious. Working with a client's images in art therapy usually involves exploring this ambiguity and amplifying the multiple meanings embodied in them.

'Gerry'

Over several years many themes and issues were touched upon and explored in my work with Gerry, a very frightened and angry young man then in his late teens. Convinced he was unlovable and uncertain of his own masculinity, Gerry felt he could never enjoy the warmth of a 'normal' human relationship. His deepest fear was that of humiliation, which, for him, was linked to the fear of being loved, as love might at any moment be withdrawn. Extreme hostility festered within Gerry as a result. This hostility, though mostly hidden, terrified Gerry and it was this that led him to seek help, firstly by asking the police, and later a psychiatrist, to lock him up.

To protect himself, Gerry cultivated an aura of mystery around himself. Nobody knew him, he had no friends and at work he cultivated a reputation as a strange, slightly menacing, 'loner'. A reputation heightened by his identification with the serial murderers Peter Sutcliffe and Dennis Nilsen, aspects of whose behaviour he began to mimic. For Gerry, it became crucial that he suppress his feelings when in the company of others and gratify these only in secret. The decision to refer Gerry for art therapy was made when it became known that one of the ways he was doing this was through drawing. Gerry referred to these drawings as his 'secret doodles' and in them he could give free reign to his troubled imagination.

Caught between the need to express and gratify his often violent and sadistic fantasy life, but fearing the consequences of doing so, Gerry found himself in a dilemma at the beginning of art therapy. As a consequence, the issue of concealment and disclosure came to play a pivotal role in our work together. Gerry frequently used visual ambiguity in order to do this, as in Figure 4.5, where words of abuse are hidden in the mist like scribble.

Many of the conflicts and difficulties that dominated Gerry's inner world found expression in his artwork through the elaborate symbol system he developed. This often combined the macabre iconography of the graveyard and horror films with more personal, fantasy based, imagery. In Figure 4.6 Gerry employed a number of symbols that had appeared in earlier images to depict his feelings about the staff of the hospital ward he was then living on.

In this image Gerry depicted something of both his internal and external world. The central figure – a knight in shining armour – represented Gerry himself, heroic, heavily defended and about to commence battle with the masked figures on the right. These more vulnerable, unarmed figures symbolised the staff group. Perched on the shoulders of the knight are two demons. These demons, Gerry told me, sought to influence his thoughts but could not be seen by

4.5 Gerry

4.6 Gerry

others, only by himself. The rearing horse on the left of the picture was similarly plagued and frightened by unseen forces. Though able to fight his human foes, his weapons and armour were, Gerry felt, of little use against the invisible, haunting demons.

At times art therapy assumed the form of an elaborate game of hide and seek or detection, as he sought to both reveal and conceal his fears and interests. Often this would involve an explicit invitation for me to decode his images, a challenge that, if indulged, I invariably got wrong. Like the hapless Dr Watson, I could never quite see all there was before me.

Freudian Symbols

Arising out of his study of dreams, Freud came to the view that, due to repression, and in order to evade censorship, the unconscious could only reveal itself indirectly through assuming a form of disguise. Freud argued that this deception was effected through metaphors and symbols (Petocz, 1999). Psychoanalytic interpretations are based on the belief that there is a discrepancy between the form of a dream or work of art – its apparent or manifest meaning – and its latent or unconscious meaning. Unfortunately, as Rycroft (1981: 73–74) comments,

> All this would be plain sailing if Freudian theory had not introduced a confusing complication by asserting that the symbols occurring in dreams differ radically from other symbols ... True symbols, in the strict psychoanalytical sense, being those which represent ideas, feelings and wishes that have been repressed. 'Only what is repressed is symbolised; only what is repressed needs to be symbolised'.[6]

From this perspective, the process of symbolisation is essentially pathological, an indication of sickness rather than health. Moreover, according to Freudian theory, the number of things needing to be symbolised is relatively small and largely restricted to family relationships, the body and sexual activity. In other words, so-called Freudian symbols function as a substitute for an object or experience. Thus the penis might be represented in a dream by objects that 'resemble it in shape – things, accordingly, that are long and up-standing, such as sticks, umbrellas, posts, trees and so on' (Freud, 1979: 188). However, because psychoanalysis is a verbal practice, difficulties arise when attempting to translate images into words. Maclagan comments,

> While Freud decries the loose, anarchic character of unconscious image-thinking, it is remarkable that nearly all examples of his interpretations of such imagery demonstrate comparatively neat and equivalent fits between a picture and some verbalisable thought. It is as though Freud believed that pictorial thinking or unconscious imagination obeyed the same rules as figurative art. (1983: 10)

As Maclagan (1983: 10) also notes, 'the Freudian model runs into severe difficulties when confronted with imagery that does not conform to these conventions'. That is to say, when faced with imagery that is non-figurative. Furthermore, by focusing its attention on what an image might be said to unconsciously represent, Freudian psychoanalysis in particular often ignores the far more interesting and pressing question of why creativity in all its various forms is so valuable and vital.

Post-Freudian Perspectives in the Nature and Function of Symbols

Enormously influential though they have undoubtedly been, Freud's views on the nature and function of symbolisation have been substantially revised by later psychoanalysts. In addition to the significant contribution made by Jung, post-Freudian psychoanalysts including Melanie Klein (1975), Marion Milner (1996), Charles Rycroft (1981), Hanna Segal (1991) and Donald Winnicott (1980), among others, have also sought to differentiate between the healthy and pathological use of symbolism. Marion Milner (1996), for example, challenged the accepted (Freudian) view of symbols as the products of repressed unconscious conflicts and anxieties. In Milner's view, regression to states of mind where thoughts and things become indistinguishable or fused, providing this is only temporary, is necessary for healthy emotional development and creativity. An essential function of art is to allow room for such illusions. For Milner, the importance of symbols resides in their capacity to transform and integrate experience.

Melanie Klein also challenged Freud's views on symbolism. In her work with children, using what she termed 'The Psycho-Analytic Play Technique', Klein recognised that the toys and art materials her young clients had access to not only represented things which interested the child in themselves, but through play they assumed a variety of symbolic meanings as well.

> Play analysis had shown that symbolism enabled the child to transfer not only interests, but also phantasies, anxieties and guilt to objects other than people. Thus a great deal of relief is experienced in play and this is one of the factors which make it so essential for the child. (Klein, in Mitchell, 1986: 52)

Through play, Klein argued, the child or playful adult was thought to be attempting to create, through the process of symbolisation, a more congenial inner world while also expressing much of the anxiety of the human situation. Although Klein approached play in a manner similar to Freud's technique of dream interpretation, she also argued that the interpretation of symbols in isolation was meaningless; 'we have to consider each child's use of symbols in connection with his particular emotions and anxieties and in relation to the whole situation which is presented in the analysis' (Klein, in Mitchell, 1986: 51). This led Klein and her followers to attach considerable importance to the process of symbol formation (see Sayers, 2000; H. Segal, 1978; J. Segal, 1992).

An inability to see our 'objects' (both people and material objects in the external world) as separate from ourselves may be indicative of serious psychological problems. The Kleinian psychoanalyst Hanna Segal explored the importance of symbolisation in relation to this (Segal, 1991). Segal drew a distinction between what she terms 'symbol formation' and the 'symbolic equation'. When we form and use symbols we substitute one thing for another, but in doing so we recognise that these things are also separate from one another. With the symbolic equation, by contrast, self and object become fused. Segal's ideas concerning the difference between *symbol formation* and the *symbolic equation* have important implications for art therapists regarding the way images are invested with meaning and are used within the therapeutic relationship. For example, not only might clay be used by a client *as if* it were shit, with all the positive or negative associations this might have for them, for some clients paint *is* shit and they would no more touch it than they would their own excrement.

What post-Freudian psychoanalysts including Klein, Milner, Segal and Winnicott have helped art therapists develop are the conceptual tools required to move beyond the interpretation of individual symbols and examine the psychological significance of the process of symbolisation in image making (see, for example Simon, 1992, 1997; Weir, 1987).

Psychoanalysis and the Interpretation of Art

While art therapists have made extensive use of psychoanalytic theory in order to further their understanding of the 'inner world' and its imaginative products, interpreting and understanding symbolic images presents particular and long-standing difficulties. Maclagan writes,

> Part of the attraction of psychoanalytic interpretation is that it has its own devious form of logic, yet is at the same time beyond normal standards of proof. By conjuring up the mirage of an alternative 'unconscious' intentionality which is in competition with consciousness, psychoanalysis (at least in its classical, Freudian forms) sets up modes of explaining a painting's hidden meaning that in effect act out a rivalry with the creative work they are purporting to analyse … the psychoanalytic privileging of depth over surface also has the effect of splitting the 'superficial' aesthetic level of a painting from its deep unconscious meaning. (2001: 13)

While offering a number of ways of understanding or interpreting images, psychoanalytic theory does not, in fact, have a monopoly on this, no matter how confidently these interpretations may be asserted. The history of art is littered with religious, mythological and allegorical symbol systems, as well as highly personal ones, which have been periodically employed to give material form to abstract ideas or states of feeling. Neither is it helpful to view the artwork produced in art therapy as merely illustrative of the repressed inner world of the artist. When the art in art therapy is viewed in this way little value is attached to the images themselves, to their emotional power, aesthetic qualities or to the context in which they were created. Rather, the image is seen in isolation and as expressing symptoms, deficits and madness in one guise or another.

Images made in art therapy may have many layers of meaning and are helpful in understanding the client's state of mind. Such meanings are, however, personal and particular even when familiar images and symbols are used. What matters most is how these images and symbols are used and understood. In art therapy the metaphorical or symbolic meaning attributed to an image must ultimately be negotiated between the art therapist and the client. To propose that an image may have a meaning other than that intended is not to replace one meaning with another, but rather to add meaning, 'A good interpretation, one could say, is something the patient can entertain in his mind. It is not a password' (Phillips, 1988: 143).

Psychoanalysis has exercised such a strong influence on art therapy mainly because it offers a ready-made language through which art therapists can both think about and articulate aspects of their work. Without this language, art therapy could not have developed in the way it has. In some respects, however, as Skaife (2001: 41) suggests, 'art therapy may be being held back by some of the language of psychoanalysis'. While this may in some ways be true, in common with developments in related disciplines like counselling and psychotherapy, art therapists have tended to 'assemble concepts and techniques into their own personal *bricolage*, thereby creating a set of interlocking local knowledges rather than a "universal" theory' (McLeod, 1997: 21). As a consequence, the dominant trend has been towards integrating psychoanalytic ideas into clinical practice rather than allowing these to dominate the process of art therapy. Nevertheless, this raises important questions concerning the extent to which art therapists might usefully draw upon psychoanalysis without doing so reductively and without neglecting the aesthetic aspects of image making (see Maclagan, 2001 for a comprehensive discussion of this issue).

Notes

1. Within contemporary psychoanalysis, and to a significant extent with art therapy too, the main theoretical model used to understand these mechanisms and processes are drawn from object-relations theory (Gomez, 1997). These theories focus upon the means by which we build up our inner world of objects from internal representations of past important relationships and experiences and the ways in which these influence, and sometimes distort, our relationships with external reality. Greenberg and Mitchell comment,

The term 'object relations theory', in its broadest sense, refers to attempts within psychoanalysis to ... confront the potentially confounding observation that people live simultaneously in an external and an internal world, and that the relationship between the two ranges from the most fluid intermingling to the most rigid separation. The term thus designates theories, or aspects of theories, concerned with exploring the relationship between real, external people and internal images and residues of relations with them … Approaches to these problems constitute the major focus of psychoanalytic theorising over the past several decades. (1983: 11–12)

2. See Mann (1991) for a thoughtful discussion of this dynamic in art therapy.

3. A well-known example of this was to be found in the imagery used in the advertising campaign for Silk Cut cigarettes.

4. As defined by Hinshelwood (1991: 32), unconscious phantasies are, 'the mental representation of those somatic events in the body which comprise the instincts, and are physical sensations interpreted as relationships with objects that cause those sensations'. Unconscious phantasies are the basic building blocks of the mind, underlie every mental process and provide both the raw material from which art is fashioned and that sustain delusions and hallucinations. Although it has been through the work of Melanie Klein and her followers that the concept of unconscious phantasy has been most extensively elaborated, as Rycroft notes, 'All schools agree that unconscious mental activity is accompanied, supported, maintained, enlivened and affected by unconscious phantasy' (1979: 118; see also J. Segal, 1985; 2000).

5. Dead metaphors are metaphors where the associations are lost or unknown. For example, although the saying 'mad as a hatter' is still widely used, its origins are obscure. The metaphor actually originates in the symptoms of St. Vitus' dance and other irrational behaviour displayed by hat makers as a result of mercury poisoning. Live metaphors, by contrast, are arresting, disruptive and have the capacity to change the way we see things.

6. It was Freud's close colleague and biographer, Ernest Jones, who originally proposed this view of symbolism in his 1916 paper 'The Theory of Symbolism' (Jones, 1916).

5

ART THERAPY IN PRACTICE

The way art therapists practice is determined by many factors. In addition to the art therapist's background, training and theoretical orientation, their practice will also be influenced by the particular needs of the client group with whom they work and by the institutional context within which this work takes place. Obvious though it may be to say so, the therapeutic needs of troubled children are often very different from those of adult psychiatric patients. Moreover, the experience of working as member of a small team providing a specialised service to a particular client group can be very different to that of working single-handed in a large organisation where the client group may be more varied. Each situation presents the art therapist with its own particular challenges, and what may be appropriate in one setting can be quite unsuitable in another. Consequently, art therapists have developed diverse ways of working according to their area of specialisation. Notwithstanding this problem, art therapists have produced guidelines for the practice of art therapy applicable to a wide range of settings. For art therapists working in the UK these are outlined in the British Association of Art Therapists' *Code of Ethics and Principles of Professional Practice* (BAAT, 1994). This document addresses a range of issues, including professional ethics, record keeping, minimum working conditions and clinical responsibility (see also Chapter 7). For many art therapists, however, putting these principles into practice can be fraught with difficulties of one kind or another and these may have a significant impact upon their work (Edwards, 1989, 1993a).

Putting Principles into Practice

Even in those situations where the work of art therapists is well understood and formally recognised as functionally different from that of other professional groups, the day-to-day task of successfully integrating art therapy into the service in which he or she is employed is always likely to prove problematic. In those situations where art therapy is not well recognised or understood, the issue of integration can be extremely difficult and the art therapist may be unable to contribute fully to the work of the organisation in which they are employed. The difficulties art therapists face in this area cannot be overcome merely by gaining professional recognition. Neither can they be explained simply in terms of theoretical differences or confusion over roles. Since art therapy is concerned with the expression of emotion, it can be perceived as threatening the status quo. The nature of the organisations in which art therapist's work will, therefore, influence their capacity to establish and maintain a credible therapeutic practice, no matter how committed or well trained they may be. This is because organisations like hospitals develop what Menzies (1977) termed 'social defence systems'. Menzies argued that social defence systems develop due to the need to create structured defence mechanisms to manage the anxiety aroused in the individual as a result of the difficult or frightening tasks they are required to undertake. In mental health this involves working closely with individuals who may be depressed, suicidal, acutely anxious or psychotic:

> A social defence mechanism develops over time as a result of the collusive interaction and agreement, often unconscious, between members of the organisation as to what form it will take. The socially structured defence mechanisms then tend to become an aspect of external reality with which old and new members of the institution must come to terms. (Menzies, 1977: 10)

Menzies' work has important implications for art therapists wishing to integrate successfully their practice into the institutions in which they work; not least through helping them understand the difficulties experienced by other groups of staff.

Practical Matters

Before it is possible to offer art therapy to clients there are a number of practical matters to which the art therapist must attend. The first of these concerns establishing an appropriate space within which art therapy may take place. As discussed in the previous chapter, this space should be sufficiently private to make image-making possible and secure enough to contain the feelings emerging as a result of this. 'Ideally', the minimum requirements to practice would consist of 'a self-contained room large enough for group work; a sink and running water, tables and chairs; a range of basic art materials; storage space, an administration area and a telephone' (BAAT, 1994).

All too frequently, however, art therapists find themselves working in conditions that are far from ideal. The art therapist may, for example, be required to run groups on wards or in other settings that limit the range or

5.1 Studio

type of art materials it is possible to use. While such limitations need not necessarily be detrimental to the art therapy process, working in this way offers a very different experience to that provided in a studio specifically dedicated to making art (see Case and Dalley, 1992; Wood, 2000 for a fuller discussion of the importance of studios in art therapy).

Because art therapy is usually provided as part of a larger service an important aspect of an art therapist's job is liaising with colleagues (psychiatrists, occupational therapists, nurses, social workers, teachers, etc.). Where art therapy is well-established there are often agreed procedures for the exchange of confidential information about clients and about developments within the service. In situations where art therapy is relatively new, establishing and accessing these information networks can be a time consuming and frustrating task. In practice, this involves attending case conferences and other meetings, and providing feedback on art therapy through writing case notes, letters and reports. Though not always the most rewarding part of an art therapist's job, these tasks are essential if colleagues are to arrive at a better understanding of art therapy, and if the art therapist is to have a say in any decisions taken concerning the care or treatment offered to clients with whom they are working.

Referral

For most clients art therapy begins following a written referral. In adult mental health this referral would usually come from the consultant psychiatrist responsible for the client's care, the decision to refer a client for art therapy having been taken after discussion at the relevant multi-disciplinary team meeting. In those instances where a client wishes to refer him or herself for art therapy, art therapists are currently advised 'that the client provides a written request for art therapy after the initial contact' (BAAT, 1994). Many art therapists use a standardised referral form to help them determine the appropriateness of the referral. In addition to providing background information such as the client's name, address and age, the referral form may also request a description of the client's problem and the reasons for their referral.

A client may be referred for art therapy for a variety of reasons. Typically, this might include a request that the art therapist,

- Help the client express feelings.
- Help them gain a better understanding of their difficulties.
- Maintain or improve the client's quality of life.

The fact that a referrer or client requests art therapy does not mean that it is necessarily appropriate to offer it. The decision to offer art therapy is normally made following an assessment.

Assessment

Once a client has been referred for art therapy they will usually be invited for an initial assessment appointment. The purpose of this meeting is to establish whether or not art therapy is the most suitable form of therapy and to arrive at a shared understanding of the problems the client wishes to address. Art therapists working in different settings, or with different client groups, may have different criteria regarding who is, and who is not, suitable for art therapy (see Case, 1998 for a discussion of the assessment process in relation to working with children). In practice, each referral is assessed on its own merits, taking into account what the client and art therapist are able to bring to the therapeutic relationship. Factors that need to be taken into account during an assessment include:

- The client's willingness to work with the available art materials.
- Whether the client is sufficiently psychologically minded to be able to reflect upon and explore the potential meaning and significance of their images.

- The client's motivation to actively participate in the resolution of their problems.
- The client's preparedness to make changes in their lives.
- An ability to tolerate frightening or troubling feelings.
- The capacity to form and sustain meaningful relationships.

During an assessment session time will usually be spent making images and discussing the client's personal history, current difficulties, and why they believe art therapy might be helpful. Offering the client the opportunity to use art materials at this stage is helpful in assessing their willingness to explore images in a metaphorical or symbolic way. The art therapist's emotional response to these images and the client's way of relating to them can provide valuable information about their difficulties and state of mind.

'Ben'

Ben referred himself for art therapy as a private, fee-paying client. Ben told me he wanted to work with an art therapist because he felt depressed and found it difficult to express himself verbally. This, he said, left him feeling frustrated and angry. Ben said that he was concerned that his anger and frustration might damage those he loved or result in his becoming depressed again. Ben told me he had received various forms of help with his depression over the years, including counselling and medication, but felt none of these had really helped him much.

At our first meeting, Ben told me he was the youngest of four children, all boys. He described his family as 'academically accomplished and competitive'. His father was a scientist, his mother a 'housewife'. Both his parents were dead; his father after a heart attack, his mother some years earlier from cancer. Ben did not have a good relationship with his father, whom he blamed for the early death of his mother and for 'forcing', him to become an academic. He described his mother as 'caring', but 'always busy', his father as 'controlling', 'irritating' and as someone who never finished anything. Ben, by contrast, proudly described himself as a 'completer/finisher' and something of a perfectionist. He did, however, acknowledge that this sometimes made him impatient with others and himself. When discussing the origin of his difficulties, Ben placed the burden of responsibility for his unhappiness on his father and more recently on his wife. It was, I felt, as though he constantly needed to blame someone or something for the dissatisfactions and imperfections in his life. When unable to do this, he blamed and punished himself.

After pursuing what he considered to be a largely unsuccessful career in teaching, Ben informed me he now earned his living as a freelance journalist. Although the income from this was irregular and often led to arguments with his wife, he nevertheless enjoyed the solitary nature of a writer's life. Writing also appeared to provide Ben with ample opportunity to have his 'say' and find relief from his conflicts. He also said he drew and painted in his spare time, 'But only as a hobby, nothing serious!' He'd thought of seeing an art therapist because he had read somewhere that Winston Churchill – one of his heroes – had painted as a form of therapy. At my suggestion, Ben brought a selection of his pictures to his first appointment. After looking through these images (mainly of landscapes and copies of paintings by old masters) I asked Ben to pick out one that he felt was particularly important to him. The image he chose was a charcoal drawing of a sea clipper (Figure 5.2).

Ben told me this drawing was a copy of a print he had hanging in his living room at home. What Ben didn't tell me at the time was that he had inherited this picture from his parents and that it had hung in a prominent position in his family home throughout his childhood. I enquired as to what it was Ben liked about the original picture and why he had chosen to copy it. Ben said he wasn't really sure what he liked about the picture, but that he'd often wished he was free to travel wherever and whenever he liked and the picture expressed something of this feeling for him. After a momentary pause Ben added that he liked the way the clipper seemed to glide over water with such ease. Looking at Ben's version of this picture a little more closely, far from gliding effortlessly over the sea, the clipper appeared to be having great difficulty ploughing through rough and choppy waters.

When I shared this observation with Ben he looked a little hurt. Clearly wounded by what he perceived to be a criticism of his artistic ability, Ben responded by saying he'd worked hard to try to get it right but that he didn't like the way he had drawn the sea and felt the picture as a whole didn't meet his expectations. Ben wondered if I had any suggestions as to how he might get it right. Politely declining his invitation I replied that whatever technical failings he felt it had, his picture seemed to exemplify something of his current state of mind and difficulties. The picture had failed to meet his expectations in much the same way that he often felt he had failed to live up to his father's expectations, no matter how hard he tried. It also seemed to me that the picture itself conveyed how he actually felt, rather than some idealised version of how things should be. The clipper, like Ben, was finding the going tough. My intention in saying this was not to discount the meaning Ben attributed to his image,

5.2 Ben

*but to open up the possibility of alternative readings and gauge his
receptiveness to these. While initially feeling troubled that his inno-
cent copy of the clipper had betrayed him by revealing more of himself than he wished it to, Ben was able to begin playing with the
metaphorical (as if) meanings carried by his image. Moving beyond
the literal, together we began to explore what the image might be saying about how it feels to be at sea in a storm, not sure of one's direction, in search of a safe anchorage and so on. This, I felt, provided
us with a sound basis on which to begin art therapy.*

Not all clients referred for art therapy are suitable. The client may, for
example, be unable or unwilling to use art as a way of exploring their difficulties, have unrealistic expectations of art therapy or be unable to form
a working relationship with the art therapist. In such circumstances the art
therapist would inform the client and the referrer of their reasons for not
offering art therapy and, where appropriate, suggest possible alternatives.

Contracting

If it is felt that art therapy is appropriate the art therapist will agree a clear
'contract' with the client or with the client's parent, legal guardian or carer.

This contract, a formal record of which will usually be added to the client's case notes, will state the reasons for offering art therapy, the type of art therapy offered, the anticipated benefits or outcomes, the number of sessions to be offered, along with other details concerning their frequency, time and location. The boundaries or ground rules of art therapy will also be discussed and agreed at this stage. In private art therapy, this will include agreeing the fee and method of payment, session times, holiday arrangements and the limits of confidentiality. It is vitally important to establish that the client is able to voluntarily agree to participate in the therapeutic process and that they understand the risks and benefits involved. In those situations where there may be some difficulty with this, as for instance with children or for individuals with learning disabilities, informed consent would be sought from a parent, guardian or the person responsible for the client's care.[1]

During the assessment process, a decision will be made as to whether the client will be offered individual or group art therapy.

Individual Art Therapy

In view of the wide variety of clients art therapists work with it is not possible to draw up a hard and fast list of criteria indicating the suitability of individual art therapy as opposed to art therapy offered in a group setting. Moreover, art therapists have often developed distinct ways of working according to their theoretical orientation, background, training and area of specialisation. This may include the acquisition of additional skills in individual or group work and this will have a bearing on the type of art therapy the art therapist is qualified to practice competently and effectively. Nevertheless, although group art therapy is widely practiced and offers a number of benefits not found in individual art therapy (see below), for many clients, and indeed for many art therapists, the latter is the modality of choice. The reasons for this are complex and varied, but the perceived advantages of individual art therapy might be said to include its flexibility, privacy and the degree of emotional intimacy offered by a one-to-one relationship. For some clients individual art therapy is indicated because their difficulties are primarily internal rather than interpersonal. For other clients it may be offered because they are considered to be too withdrawn or vulnerable to participate fully in a group.

Depending upon the art therapist's assessment of the client's difficulties, individual art therapy may be provided on a long-term or short-term basis. Definitions of long-term and short-term therapy vary, but the former may be conducted over a number of years, whereas the latter may range from a single session to 12 or more. Generally speaking, clients with enduring or complex difficulties will be offered longer-term work. Short-term art therapy may be more appropriate where there is a clear focus to the client's problem, as is the case for client's who have suffered a recent bereavement and where there are no major complications in the grieving process. Unfortunately, due to the pressure to reduce costs and the length of waiting lists, many art therapists are unable to offer long-term individual art therapy even where this is clearly indicated.

Group Art Therapy

Group art therapy can be used with a wide range of clients for whom individual work may not be appropriate or for whom being in a group offers significant benefits (Greenwood and Layton, 1987; Huet, 1997; Skaife, 1990; Strand, 1990; see also Liebmann, 1990, 1999; Waller, 1993; Skaife and Huet, 1998). Group art therapy may, for example, be more suitable for clients who are unable to cope with the intimacy of a one-to-one relationship or whose difficulties are most apparent in social situations. Drawing upon a range of sources, but particularly the work of Yallom (1970), Waller (1993: 35–36) identifies nine curative factors in group therapy, including the sharing of information, the instillation of hope, catharsis and interpersonal learning. To this list Waller adds a further 13 curative factors to be found within what she terms 'group interactive art therapy', although many of these are also applicable to individual art therapy. Central to the model of group interactive art therapy is the importance attached to the role of image making in stimulating creativity and facilitating interaction between group members and the art therapist:

> The group process may be intensified through the introduction of art materials. A feature of using art therapy as part of a group process is that processes may develop very quickly, and are made visible, more tangible and available for working on. (Waller, 1993: 40)

Within art therapy there are a number of different approaches to group art therapy. These include 'open' and 'closed' groups, 'directive' or theme based groups (Liebmann, 1999; Silverstone, 1997) and 'non-directive' groups. Within the latter category are models of art therapy identified in the literature as group analytic art therapy (McNeilly, 1984, 1987), group interactive art therapy (Waller, 1993) and art psychotherapy groups (Skaife and Huet, 1998). These different models of art therapy group practice can, as Skaife and Huet (1998: 10) comment, 'be distinguished by the relationship of pictures to words or verbal interaction within them'.

Open Groups

The studio based open group could, as Case and Dalley (1992: 196) suggest, be described as 'the classic form of art therapy', having its 'antecedents in the atelier, studio or workshop of artistic tradition'. This tradition has long played an essential part in the education of artists and shaped the way many early art therapists approached their work with clients (see, for example, Adamson, 1990; Lyddiatt, 1971; Thomson, 1997). As discussed in Chapter 3, during the pioneering phase of art therapy's development in the UK, the studio often functioned as an asylum within an asylum, offering a quiet, private space where patients could become absorbed in the process of making art in the presence of others (Wood, 2000). Groups of patients would attend the studio or art therapy department, often on an informal basis, to make images and objects for a whole morning or afternoon. In studio based open art therapy groups it is the art that is very much regarded as the therapeutic medium, not the group itself. As such, the focus tends to be more on the individual within the group rather than with the group process. Although the promotion of community care policies in the UK during the 1980s led to the loss of many of the large studio environments in which art therapy first developed, the tradition of offering open, studio based art therapy continues, albeit in a modified form. As Deco (1998: 106) suggests, providing the open group has firmly established boundaries, this model of art therapy 'provides the flexibility and containment necessary to work with the diversity of often highly disturbed patients that are found within the acute psychiatric setting and to accommodate short-term contact'.

Closed Groups

From the 1970s onwards, the informality of the studio based open art therapy groups began to be replaced by the increasing use of closed art therapy groups. These groups would usually be comprised of a fixed membership drawn from a defined client group and run for a specified length of time. These closed groups might, for example, be offered to selected members of a particular ward or unit as part of a treatment or rehabilitation programme. This development in art therapy practice was in response to a number of factors:

- The developing awareness by art therapists of the influence group dynamics had upon their work.
- The creation of art therapy posts in the community and the widening of the client groups with whom art therapists worked.
- The influence of ideas on the therapeutic potential of group work, including those drawn from the human potential movement in the USA and group analysis in the UK.
- The use of group therapy methods in art therapy training (see Chapter 6).
- The developing professionalism of art therapy. As previously noted, in the UK this trend included emphasising what was different about art therapy and an increasing rigour with regard to theory and clinical practice.

While the foregoing factors combined to foster a climate of diversity and creativity within group based approaches to art therapy, they also generated conflict and controversy. During the 1980s differences surfaced within art therapy regarding the use of themes.

Using Themes

In the kind of closed groups described above the group would often work to a set theme or on a group painting, this task having been chosen and introduced by the art therapist with the aim of facilitating creative activity. Although the length of each phase might vary depending on the membership and nature of the group, the typical format for such a group session would involve the art therapist introducing the chosen theme, followed by a period of activity (painting, modelling, etc.). The session would conclude with a discussion during which the group members would share their images along with any thoughts and feelings they may have in response to these. Because it is usually the art therapist who chooses the theme, it tends to be the case that this discussion is mainly between the art therapist and individual members of the group.

In the UK, the best known advocate of this structured or directive approach to art therapy is Marian Liebmann, whose book *Art Therapy for Groups* (1999) contains an extensive collection of themes, art based games and exercises. One example is an exercise titled 'Gifts':

> Make, draw or paint gifts you would like to give each person in the group, then give them … Discussion will explore feelings around giving and receiving, and possibly around parting with the gifts.
>
> Variations:
>
> (a) To end a group, a 'goodbye' gift to take away.
> (b) Can be geared to festivals, e.g. Christmas, Easter, etc.
> (c) Stipulate kind of gift – concrete, abstract, etc. … (Liebmann, 1999: 174)

The rationale for using structured art groups is that this way of working may help people who have difficulty using art for self-exploration and that it provides a non-threatening means of fostering co-operation between group members. This approach is not, however, without its difficulties:

> If used inappropriately, some themes can evoke feelings which are too much for that group to handle at that time. At the other end of the spectrum, some can lead to a superficial experience which leaves people dissatisfied. (Liebmann, 1999: 12)

Nevertheless, as Liebmann (1999: 12) also states, 'Between these two poles there is a wide variety of group experiences using art structures which can be interesting and revealing, and also enjoyable'.

While the theme based approach to group work has its advocates, it also has its critics. McNeilly (1983, 1984, 1987), for example, casts doubt on the therapeutic value of 'directive' art therapy groups, and suggests that among the negative consequences of this approach to group art therapy are 'catharsis of questionable long-term value; intolerance of the uncovered feelings, and withdrawal or flight from the group' (1984: 204); he also suggests 'that the process of introducing themes into an art group is a forced entry into the group, leading to ever-increasing demands from the members and severely restricting intragroup relationships' (1984: 205).

For McNeilly it is vitally important that images and themes emerging in analytic art therapy groups are firmly rooted in the dynamics of the group. At times this may lead to the spontaneous production of images that are similar in form or content and which can be understood as an expression of the shared experience of the group. McNeilly (1987) uses the term 'resonance' to describe this phenomenon (see also Roberts, 1984). The art therapist's role in the group is analogous to that of an orchestra's conductor (McNeilly, 1987: 9). This approach requires that the art therapist keep their interventions to a minimum in order to avoid dependency and allow the group to develop its own healing capacity.

In practice, many art therapists have developed ways of working that combine a theme based approach with an awareness of group dynamics (Greenwood and Layton, 1987). As Skaife and Huet (1998: 10) comment, this flexibility within contemporary art therapy group practice 'means that art therapists are able to adapt to the needs of different client groups and offer therapeutic resources to people who otherwise would be unable to use purely verbal therapy'.

One session in the life of an adolescent art therapy group

The young people who attended this session assembled in the waiting area prior to entering the art room. Once the young people had entered the art room and settled I began the session by explaining that I had decided to exclude Robert from the group because of his disruptive behaviour in the previous session. After a brief discussion about this, the theme for the current session was explained. It was suggested that the group paint whatever they wished for two minutes using the finger-paint available in the centre of the table. In addition to this, I introduced a rule that only one finger be used, the aim being to introduce a degree of frustration into the activity as a way of taking up the issue of the impatience to get on with things previously expressed by many of the young people in the group.

As the first working period began Susan excused herself from the group saying she was going to the toilet. Diane followed her shortly afterwards, having made only a brief start on her picture. Diane's departure was quickly followed by that of Neil, who said the thought of using finger-paint made him feel sick. Neither Susan, Diane or Neil returned to the group. Although she did not return to the group on this occasion, in the following session Susan, who had been a member of the art therapy group for some time, was able to tell the group that she had found it impossible to stay in the art room because so many new people had joined and she felt excluded.

The first exercise was then repeated, adding an extra finger at each successive stage until the young people were able to use the whole of one hand to work with. Before this final stage was reached Will and David, evidently unable to contain their impatience, began smearing paint over each other. Though their behaviour was more playful than aggressive, it began to alarm and trouble the rest of the group. When the exercise was finished the materials were cleared away, hands were washed and the pictures put to one side. Time was then allowed for the young people to discuss their feelings or pictures. As might have been anticipated with so many new members having joined the group, none of them expressed a wish to talk about their images or themselves.

Before the second exercise was explained a large sheet of paper was placed in the centre of the table. The young people were then asked to think about situations like the one they now found themselves in. Jean likened the group to the daily community meeting held in the unit which all the young people were expected to attend. As others in the group indicated they were in agreement with this comparison it was suggested that they use the finger-paint to depict their feelings about the community meeting. The underlying aim throughout the previous sessions had been to develop the group in such a way as to enable the group to allow their own feelings to emerge and for them to have a range of skills available to them for those feelings to find an appropriate form of expression.

The picture developed tentatively in the initial stages with the group being reluctant to extend their contributions away from the area immediately in front of them. In the contributions I made to the picture I made a deliberate point of using the whole of the paper and of moving around the table, thereby offering an alternative model of behaviour. After ten minutes Pat, who had become increasingly restless, suddenly left the room and could not be persuaded to return. Jean said a big flag should be put up in the middle of the community meeting picture, but after giving the idea more thought decided to place this in her area of the picture. After doing this Jean retreated from the activity and made no further contribution to it, eventually leaving the group about ten minutes later.

A short time after Jean left, June and Paul entered the art room to ask what was happening and permission to join in. After consulting the group permission was given. As the picture progressed it became increasingly messy and chaotic. Paul, with support and encouragement from Steven, painted over the area Ravi had been working on; an obvious attack that was noted and commented upon. At which point he too lost interest. Steven occupied himself by mockingly writing the word 'FEEL' over as much of the picture as he could. Meanwhile June confined herself to a small area of the picture and mixed colours into each other until they were blended into a brown colour that she said looked like dog shit.

After the working period was over, the group re-assembled to talk about the session. Although they were again reluctant to share their thoughts and feelings, Paul commented that the picture looked and felt messy. Steven asked if the picture could be put up in the community room. While stating that this wouldn't be appropriate, I enquired how Steven might feel if the picture was displayed where everyone could see it. Steven said he wouldn't like it because it was so messy. Paul then suggested the group could do another one, only properly. After asking him what he meant by this he said one that was 'not so messy'.

Difficult though the session had at times been, it did allow many of the issues and conflicts with which the young people were struggling at the time to emerge in a reasonably safe and contained way. The messiness of the group painting was an accurate description of the way community meetings often felt at that time. It also provided an accurate representation of the dynamics of the group itself, particularly the need for safety, the sense of inner messiness experienced by the members of the group and the difficulties associated with rivalry, control, power and dominance.

Art Therapy in Practice

The client groups with whom art therapists work include individuals of all ages and who may have learning difficulties (Rees, 1998; Tipple 1992, 1993, 1994), physical illnesses (Knight, 1987; Malachiodi, 1999a, 1999b; Pratt and Wood, 1998; Skaife, 1993), addictions (Waller and Mahoney, 1998) or other mental health problems; including autism (Evans and Dubowski, 2001), eating disorders (Levens, 1995; Rust, 1987, 1992; Schaverien, 1989; M. Wood, 1996) and psychosis (Killick, 1991, 1993; Killick and Schaverien, 1997). Of all the mental health problems art therapists are likely to encounter in their clinical work, depression is by far the most common and familiar. According to the mental health charity MIND,

> Depression with anxiety is experienced by 9.2 per cent of people in Britain, and depression without anxiety by 2.8 per cent. Overall, depression occurs in 1 in 10 adults or 10 per cent of the population in Britain at any one time … Estimates of lifetime prevalence vary from 1 in 6 to 1 in 4. A summary of studies on more severe depression gives a figure of 1 in 20 people at any one time who suffer major or 'clinical' depression.[2]

It is important to acknowledge that depression is part of the experience of every human being. As Storr contends,

> There is no hard and fast line to be drawn between depression of a kind which we all experience in response to loss, and the kind of depression which is labelled a psychiatric illness and which requires psychiatric treatment. Depression varies enormously in depth and severity, but not in its essential nature. (1990: 143–144)

The experience of depression is characterised by feelings of sadness, loss of interest and enjoyment in life, fatigue and a lack of motivation, feelings of uselessness, inadequacy, worthlessness or guilt (Rowe, 1978, 1984; Wolpert, 1999). It is often through metaphors and images that clients are best able to convey their experience of depression. In the Foreword to Dorothy Rowe's book *The Experience of Depression* (1978) Bannister observes,

> In our attempts to convey to each other our personal experience of depression we have called upon every kind of metaphor. We have drawn analogies from disease and injury – to be sick at heart, to suffer a broken heart. We enter 'the doldrums', the area where no wind of hope or purpose moves us. Depression preys on our mind, we sink into it, we are downcast, we are crestfallen, bowed down, cut up, careworn. Even if we seek the company of others we are the skeleton at the feast. The very vision of the world becomes our metaphor when we experience the 'blackness' of despair.

The bleak sense of inner desolation, alienation, failure and persecutory guilt often experienced by individuals suffering from depression was depicted with great clarity by 'Danny'.

'Danny'

Danny, a young man in his early twenties, was referred for art therapy shortly after his admission to hospital following an overdose. This overdose, not his first, was preceded by a long period of heavy drinking, bouts of depression and failing his college exams. It was thought that Danny might benefit from art therapy because he had

5.3 Danny

5.4 Danny

difficulties communicating with his family and with the ward staff. It was also hoped that art therapy might help him express his feelings and gain some insight into his difficulties. At the time I first *met him, Danny was able to offer little more than monosyllabic 'yes'/'no' answers to any question put to him and found it virtually impossible to initiate a conversation. In stark contrast to his withdrawn behaviour, Danny's images were, from the very beginning, powerfully expressive of his inner world.*

Danny settled quickly into attending the Art Therapy Department as a regular member of an open art therapy group and over many months produced a considerable body of work. The despair and isolation Danny felt, along with a considerable amount of his anger and self-hatred, was expressed through his imagery. Almost all his artwork was figurative, carefully executed and depicted scenes of brutality, persecution, destruction, decay and loneliness. In contrast to this, Danny's demeanour was mild-mannered and he rarely revealed even the briefest glimpse of the violence found in his images.

One way of thinking about Danny's images is that they depicted a state of mind described in the psychoanalytic literature as characteristic of the 'depressive position'; wherein,

All one's loved ones within are dead and destroyed, all goodness is dispersed, lost, in fragments, wasted and scattered to the winds; nothing is left within but utter desolation. Love brings sorrow and sorrow brings guilt, the intolerable tension mounts, there is no escape, one is utterly alone, there is no one to share or help. (Riviere, in Rowe, 1978: 8)[3]

Clients may experience and express similar feelings in art therapy. When this is the case, as it was for Danny, it is often because the client believes his or her hateful feelings have destroyed all that they love, and, as a consequence, experience an acute sense of loss and guilt. Difficult though they may be to tolerate, these feelings can give rise to a desire to restore and recreate that which clients feel they have lost or destroyed. Hanna Segal writes,

The artist's need is to recreate what he feels in the depths of his internal world. It is his inner perception of the deepest feeling of the depressive position that his internal world is shattered which leads to the necessity for the artist to recreate something that is felt to be a whole new world. (1991: 86)

Within the psychoanalytic literature the term 'reparation' is used to describe this process.[4]

The story that slowly emerged during the time I worked with Danny was that as a child he had suffered from bed-wetting and also had problems controlling his bowels. This resulted in his spending a considerable amount of time in hospital; an experience he found terrifying as he couldn't understand what was happening to him.

*Danny also suffered further humiliation at school where he was
bullied, he said, by both teachers and pupils alike. These experiences
left him feeling shamed, angry, helpless and lonely.*

Woodmansey (1989) offers some helpful insights into the way external
conflict is internalised and ultimately leads to the formation, in the inner
world, of a 'punitive' or 'humiliating' superego (see also Roth, 2001).

The term 'superego' (which should perhaps be replaced by 'anti-ego') is used to
denote a set of habitual response tendencies that are antagonistic to the self, and
cause the subject to behave as if he were two separate persons at war with each
other. The superego develops in early life and may be 'punitive' or 'humiliating'
or both. The former kind arises through learning to restrain the self from dangerously rebelling against overwhelming coercion, and the latter through intensive striving to avoid parental scorn. The resultant 'internal' conflict resembles
the external one between an actual child and a demanding parent; and the
relative fortunes of the two antagonists provide a model for understanding the
characteristics of many kinds of emotional and psychosomatic disorder.
(Woodmansey, 1989: 26)

Repeated experiences of humiliation during childhood of the kind Danny
was subjected to may, in later life, be re-experienced internally as a crush-
ing defeat by the superego resulting in all the feeling states commonly
associated with depression, including self-hatred. Moreover, being obedient, in order to prevent punishment or humiliation, may result in a com-
pulsion to obey the dictates of the superego and thus avoid feelings of guilt
or shame.

Some parents press their children to extreme standards of conduct, achievement
or self-denial, by imbuing them with their own contempt or condemnation of
people who fail to reach those standards. Such a child will learn that, if he does
not succeed, he can expect to lose the security or self-esteem derived from feeling approved of and valued by his parents. (Woodmansey, 1989: 28)

This appeared to be very much the case for Danny. For no matter how hard
he tried he could not achieve the control of his bodily functions demanded
of him. Neither could he challenge his persecutors. Experience had taught
him that to do so merely invited further punishment or humiliation.

*In addition, and due mainly to conflicts within his family, Danny
had never been able to establish a secure and stable relationship
with either parent, despite having made repeated attempts to do so.
Throughout his life, Danny had been told how unlovable, inadequate
or incompetent he was. As might perhaps be expected, this resulted
in Danny developing a self-image as someone unlovable and
unwanted, and a view of others as unavailable and rejecting.
Danny's belief that he could never form or sustain relationships
based on genuine affection had resurfaced while at college, resulting
in angry and unfounded accusations regarding his girlfriend's*

unfaithfulness. These accusations placed enormous strain on the relationship, leading to its eventual breakdown, the onset of Danny's depression and his eventual admission to hospital. The breakdown of his first 'serious' adult relationship served to confirm his fear that he was unlovable. It also reinforced his tendency to interpret any loss as yet another example of his failure to make satisfactory relationships with others. Once given form, these fears, and the thoughts and feelings that sustained them, became the focus of art therapy.

For Danny, the images he made in art therapy served two main purposes. Firstly, they helped him tell his story, albeit in a fragmentary form. Through the process of making them, Danny's images also afforded him the opportunity to begin to make sense of his experiences. As Storr puts it,

> The creative process can be a way of protecting the individual against being overwhelmed by depression; a means of regaining a sense of mastery in those who have lost it, and, to a varying extent, a way of repairing the self damaged by bereavement or by the loss of confidence in human relationships which accompanies depression from whatever cause. (1990: 143)

The Triangular Relationship Revisited

In Chapter 1 it was stated that the therapeutic process in art therapy is primarily concerned with the dynamic interaction between the client, the artwork and the art therapist. This relationship is often referred to as the triangular relationship (Case, 1990, 2000; Schaverien, 1990, 2000; Wood, 1990). Within the triangular relationship the interaction between the client and their artwork, or between the client and the art therapist, may be in the foreground or background at different points in time. During an art therapy session it may be the therapeutic benefits derived from image making that are of paramount importance for the client. At other times, it is the relationship with the art therapist, mediated through image making, which assumes a central role. For the art therapist, there are a number of issues to consider in relation to this dynamic. These include maintaining appropriate boundaries and a respectful acceptance of the client and their images. Facilitating the emergence of images that assume an expressive or communicative function also requires the art therapist to listen, look, think and respond appropriately.

The kinds of things an art therapist might pay attention to during a session include:

- *The main themes to emerge during the session and how these were responded to.* If these themes emerged spontaneously they may have considerable significance for the individual or the group. They may, for example, indicate the emergence of new material or the re-working of existing issues.

- *The materials the client used.* Where clients have access to a wide range of art materials (including wet and dry media, different kinds and sizes of paper, clay and other 3-D media) their choice of materials may have particular significance. So too might a change from using paint to clay, from making small images to larger ones or from working in representational (figurative) to a non-figurative (abstract) manner.
- *How the client used the art materials.* Clients in art therapy may have very different ways of working (slowly, rapidly, messily, repetitively, etc.) and this may be indicative of their current state of mind. The way paint has been applied (thickly or thinly, for example), the quality of mark making (heavy or light), or the particular use of colour, shape and texture may also reveal something of this.
- *The client's approach to the image making process.* For some clients seen in art therapy this may vary considerably within a session or over time. Sometimes the client may be prolifically productive, whereas at other times they may be blocked or unable work at all.

In considering these, and other issues emerging in their work with clients, the art therapist's thinking will be guided by both their emotional response to the client's behaviour and images, and by theoretical ideas drawn from a variety of sources.

Endings

Ending therapy raises many issues (Edwards, 1997; Murdin, 2000). From the very beginning of therapy both the client and the art therapist are inexorably moving towards ending and parting. It is towards the making of a satisfactory ending in order to make a new beginning that the process of therapy is directed. Perhaps the most powerful feelings touched upon during the ending phase of art therapy are those associated with loss. The link between ending and loss is a potent one, especially if the feelings aroused by previous losses were experienced as traumatic or overwhelming. An ending experienced as a loss may leave the client feeling bereft, vulnerable or needy. As art therapy draws to a close, feelings of anger, rejection or abandonment experienced by the client in response to previous losses may be triggered. Similar feelings may also be experienced by the client at the end of each session or before a break in therapy. For some clients, therefore, ending may prove particularly difficult and requires patience and humility on the part of the therapist (Wood, 1990).

Ending art therapy usually represents a compromise between hoped for changes and the limitations within which the client and art therapist have been working. Ideally, the decision to end therapy is one mutually agreed by both therapist and client. In time-limited art therapy, this decision may have been taken at the very beginning of therapy. In those situations where art therapy is more open ended the decision to end therapy is taken when the agreed aims of art therapy have been met. In either case, both parties will have been working towards closure for some time prior to the actual ending. Sometimes, however, therapy ends in circumstances that are far from ideal. The art therapist may leave because they are changing jobs, or the client may suddenly stop attending sessions. A central dilemma often facing the client during the process of ending is that therapy involves change, and change requires that the client give something up, 'be this a symptom, a habitual behaviour, an attitude of mind, a value system or a particular form of relationship to another person ... change is thus desired and at the same time feared and resisted (Wolff, 1977: 11). The feelings generated by this dilemma can be extremely powerful and can lead the client to act out in order to avoid experiencing them; possibly resulting in a premature ending.

'Nicki'

For Nicki, who had a history of beginning but then abruptly ending therapy, help was longed for but also feared. Socially isolated and often immersed in a world of fantasy, Nicki craved emotional intimacy but also feared this, believing she would lose her identity if others got too close. Even having the opportunity to express her feelings was experienced as a potential loss. Endings, by contrast, were experienced as a rejection. For much of her adult life Nicki had, with increasing desperation, attempted to manage her fear of intimacy and abandonment by avoiding either. To avert the feelings of rejection she associated with ending, Nicki would often attempt to extend the time boundaries of the session by refusing to leave or, believing I would forget about her, by seeking to contact me between appointments through phoning or writing letters. At other times, Nicki would take away her work or leave sessions early. In each case, her behaviour appeared to be intended to avoid the fear of leaving something of herself behind or the pain of rejection. Although this dynamic was explored in therapy, it was not, regrettably, possible to help Nicki overcome her fears and art therapy ended prematurely.

The ambivalent feelings clients have about ending often find expression through the way images made in art therapy are disposed of.

Disposal

The question of what happens to the artworks after art therapy has ended is a complex one. It is, moreover, one that is self evidently not restricted to the issue of ending therapy. Clients dispose of their images and artworks during or after sessions by all manner of means and for all manner of reasons; including hostility, the need for containment, or through a desire to have the artwork – and, by inference, the person who made it – valued. The fate of an image after the session has ended, or after therapy has ended, may, therefore, involve its being displayed, offered as a gift, or possibly being destroyed. In each case, the fate of the image or object has meaning and significance.

> A picture may be kept by the client, left with the therapist, or a conscious decision may be made to destroy the pictures. The point is that, when these decisions are consciously arrived at, in negotiation with the therapist, they may be important markers for acknowledging the importance of the ending of therapy. (Schaverien, 1992: 115)

More often than not clients dispose of their artwork by leaving it with the art therapist. Sometimes these artworks are left with the explicit intention of being collected or returned to at a later date. At other times they may be forgotten or abandoned, the process of making images in art therapy having served its purpose. The advice provided by BAAT on this issue in the *Code of Ethics and Principles of Professional Practice for Art Therapists* is that,

> All material produced during the art therapy session should be named, dated and safely stored during the therapeutic relationship. Problems of storage may need to be addressed in the case of long-term clients, but in general it is advisable that material and case notes should be kept for a minimum of three years. (BAAT, 1994)

Painful though ending art therapy may sometimes be, it is essential that clients are able to consciously accept the reality of this. The images clients make in therapy may help them successfully negotiate the transitional period between the end of therapy and their acceptance of the reality of this ending. These images may, in time, be forgotten, destroyed or disposed of in some other way. But during this period of transition they can provide considerable comfort and reassurance to the client. Though it is difficult to define precisely what a good or satisfactory ending might entail, it is, perhaps, one in which feelings of sadness and anger, along with those of gratitude, may be expressed and acknowledged as fully as possible.

Notes

1. Information concerning the UK Department of Health guidelines on informed consent are available at www.doh.gov.uk/consent/index.htm
2. Statistics concerning the prevalence of mental distress in the UK vary. The Office for National Statistics (previously the Office for Population and Census surveys or OPCS) puts the figure at one in six adults at any one time (Office of

National Statistics, 2000). In the age group 16 to 19 years it is believed that 6 per cent of boys and 16 per cent of girls have some form of mental health problem and that 2 per cent of children under the age of 12 have some form of depression, compared to 5 per cent of teenagers (Mental Health Foundation, 1999). A useful source of statistics on mental health in the UK can be found at www.mind.org.uk/ Information/Factsheets/statistics/ from where this quotation is reproduced.

3. As defined by Rycroft (1979: 32) the depressive position is 'reached by the infant (or by the patient in analysis) when he realises that both his love and hate are directed towards the same object – the mother – becomes aware of his ambivalence and is concerned to protect her from his hate and to make reparation for what damage he imagines he has done'.

4. See Glover (2000), Hinshelwood (1991), H. Segal (1978, 1991) and J. Segal (1992) for a further discussion of reparation in relation to creativity.

6

TRAINING: FROM APPRENTICE TO PRACTITIONER

The History of Art Therapy Training In The UK

Although the question of what kind of training an art therapist should receive was a matter of some debate during the 1950s and early 1960s, it was not until the formation of the British Association of Art Therapists in 1963 that the task of devising suitable programmes of training began to receive serious attention (Waller, 1992). During the following decade a number of trainings in art therapy began to develop which, although having many common elements, also had notable differences in emphasis. For example, in 1969 an option in art therapy had been introduced into the Postgraduate Certificate in Education (PGCE) course at the School of Art Education in Birmingham (Byrne, 1980), and in 1970 a Certificate in Remedial Art course had begun at St Albans School of Art (Evans, 1979). In 1974 Goldsmiths College in London introduced an option in art therapy to its PGCE course (Waller, 1979). By the late 1970s the courses at both Goldsmiths College and (then) Hertfordshire College of Art and Design (now the University of Hertfordshire) had been converted into full-time Postgraduate Diploma in Art Therapy courses. Regrettably, the course at Birmingham Polytechnic failed in its attempt to become a discrete Postgraduate Diploma in Art Therapy and had DHSS approval withdrawn in 1985 (Donnelly, 1984).

As the differences in emphasis between the three then centres of art therapy training have been written about elsewhere I shall not attempt to describe them in detail here; see Waller (1991, 1992a). It is, however, necessary to acknowledge that two of the art therapy training courses were initially offered as an integral part of an art teacher training course, while the course at St Albans School of Art was intended to equip those offered places on it (including nurses, occupational therapists and other health care professionals, as well as artists) with the necessary practical and theoretical skills relevant to the practice of art therapy. This practice was also seen as being an 'essentially Health Service orientated activity ... concerned with working with the mentally ill and handicapped' (Evans, 1979: 4). Thus a split existed between those trainings which were allied to, and clearly identified with, art education, and the St Albans course which courted academic approval through its links with the medical profession.

One significant feature of these differences in emphasis within the training courses was that they reflected conflicting views within the emerging profession of art therapy itself. Many of the more prominent art therapists at the time were strongly influenced by the anti-psychiatry movement and were consequently 'reluctant to see art therapy being allied to psychiatry' (Waller, 1992a: 214). Tensions in the relationship between art therapy and psychiatry have, as previously noted, shaped the development of the profession in a number of ways, both positive and negative. At the heart of this issue, especially during the developmental phase of art therapy training, was the question of professional autonomy. That is to say, whether or not the training art therapists received should equip artists to work as independent therapists, or whether other health care professionals, without necessarily possessing a background in the visual arts, could be trained in the therapeutic application of art as an adjunct to the work of more established professional groups like psychiatrists or clinical psychologists. The development of art therapy training in the UK and in other countries has been of crucial importance in resolving this matter (see Chapter 8).

The Role of the British Association of Art Therapists Registration and Education Sub-Committee

In an attempt to reconcile the differences between the training institutions, along with other issues concerned with art therapy training – primarily that an understanding of artistic practice was seen as central to such a training, not an optional extra – the British Association of Art Therapists established a Registration and Education Sub-Committee in 1976. The committee consisted of representatives from the three existing training courses, along with a number of practising art therapists, and had the aim of arriving at a 'core course', which all the training institutions would be required to deliver. This step was fundamental in establishing a unified and coherent profession. The recommendations made by the committee stipulated:

- That entry to training should be at postgraduate level, with intending students 'normally' having a first degree or its equivalent in the visual arts.
- That the training should consist of a balance of theoretical, clinical and experiential learning.

- And that students must 'spend at least 60 days on placement in appropriate institutions under the supervision of persons with responsibility for the clinical application of art therapy' (BAAT, 1978).

The 'core course criteria' drawn up by BAAT and the art therapy courses in 1978 were subsequently approved by the Department of Health and Social Security in 1982 as an appropriate training for art therapists employed in the NHS. These criteria continued to determine the nature and duration of the training art therapists received until the mid-1990s. However, from the mid-1980s, the British Association of Art Therapists, and representatives from those academic institutions which trained art therapists (including, from 1984 onwards, the University of Sheffield) initiated, through BAAT's Training and Education Committee, a review of the existing core course criteria. This process culminated in 1992 with the adoption of revised Core Course requirements for postgraduate art therapy training (BAAT, 1992a).

The 'Core Course Criteria' for Art Therapy Training in the UK

Though retaining many of the criteria for training previously listed – that, for example, training should continue to be at a postgraduate level – the revised core course requirements contained a number of significant differences.

- That only nationally validated institutions of Higher Education are appropriate venues for art therapy training.
- That training should be rooted in psychotherapeutic concepts.
- That the length of training should increase from one year full time to two years full time or its part time equivalent.
- That the length of the clinical placement should be increased from a minimum of 60 days to a minimum of 120 days.
- And that for the duration of the course each trainee must undertake some form of personal therapy on a minimum basis of one session per week. (BAAT, 1992a)

A notable anomaly arising from these changes was that the academic qualification awarded on successful completion of the extended training remained that of a Postgraduate Diploma. At the present time a number of the UK art therapy courses are in the process of increasing the academic content of the training with a view to awarding a degree at MA level following an additional period of research-based study.

Currently there are six postgraduate training courses approved and accredited by the British Association of Art Therapists. These are based at Queen's University Belfast; the University of Derby; Queen Margaret College in Edinburgh; the University of Hertfordshire; Goldsmiths College,

University of London and the University of Sheffield. See Appendix 2 for further information about these courses. The Postgraduate Diploma awarded by these courses is recognised by the Health Professions Council as entitling the holder to apply for state registration (see Chapter 7).

Training as an Art Therapist

As art therapy established itself as a profession, interest in it as a possible career option for arts graduates has resulted in a significant increase in both the number of training courses available nationally, and in the number of enquiries and applications for places on these courses. The motives applicants have for wishing to train as art therapists vary, as do their age, personal qualities and background. It is difficult, therefore, to generalise about this, although many applicants are attracted to the profession because they have found image making helpful in gaining a better understanding of their own emotional conflicts, as well as those of clients. Successful applicants for art therapy training courses are usually fine art graduates who are able to demonstrate a sound understanding of, and commitment to, the practice of visual art. Only in very exceptional circumstances are other qualifications accepted.

The insistence that applicants have acquired this background in the visual arts prior to training has been, as Waller (1991: 256) acknowledges, 'fundamental in defining art therapy as a 'profession' rather than an occupation or a craft'. As Case and Dalley (1992: 148) comment, 'Without this foundation, the art base of the profession of art therapy is eroded'. Despite being subject to criticism – that, for instance, it is merely a matter of political expediency or that arts graduates may be overly concerned with the formal qualities of an image rather than its psychological content (see Birtchnell, 1986) – this stance is important for two main reasons.

Firstly, a background in art is important in that it helps students to begin applying their familiarity with art and image making in therapeutic relationships from the outset of their training. In addition to having acquired an in-depth knowledge of art media and materials, along with a familiarity with the dynamics of the creative process, graduates from fine art courses in the UK also tend to be independently minded and socially aware. The kind of education typically provided on an undergraduate fine art course is certainly very different from that on offer to most medical and paramedical students. Nevertheless, while acknowledging the importance of gaining a grounding in the visual arts prior to training, one of the ironies of art education in the UK is that fine art students are often actively discouraged from using their art for anything remotely resembling self-exploration. Many do, of course, but this is frequently unrecognised or unacknowledged (Rawcliffe, 1987).

The second reason a sound understanding of the visual arts was considered important is that many art therapists felt, and continue to feel, that this commitment to art was essential in ensuring that art therapy 'offered an "alternative" view of treatment to the prevailing "medical" model' (Waller, 1991: 256). Having gained a degree of understanding of the cultural context, traditions, technical and psychological processes operative in making and responding to art through their undergraduate education, art therapists are generally less inclined to view the images made by clients in purely psychological or diagnostic terms than their medical colleagues.

In addition to having a grounding in the visual arts, those accepted onto the art therapy training courses are usually mature, flexible people who have substantial experience in the therapeutic application of visual art and of working in mental health, education, special needs, or social services prior to training. As most art therapy students will normally need to fund part or all of their training themselves, they also need to be resourceful. While many of the applicants for the Postgraduate Diploma courses possess the foregoing qualifications and personal qualities, their familiarity with art therapy itself is often limited. For some, reading around the subject or talking to art therapists about their work fills this gap. Others may have attended talks, workshops or art therapy 'schools'. Both kinds of experience may have led directly to the decision to train. In recent years the need for opportunities to acquire a fuller appreciation of art therapy, both experientially and theoretically, has provided the impetus for the development of introductory or Foundation in Art Therapy courses. In addition to providing a good grounding in the subject for individuals intending to pursue a career in art therapy, these introductory courses have also proved to be popular with those working in other professions who are interested in finding out more about the theory and practice of art therapy (see Dudley et al., 1998) for a thoughtful discussion of the kind of issues touched upon and explored on such courses.

The Aims Of Art Therapy Training

The principle aim of the training offered through the postgraduate Diploma courses is 'to enable graduates to undertake the clinical practice of Art Therapy in which visual art and the process of making images play a central role in the context of the psychotherapeutic relationship (BAAT, 1992a)'.

In practice, training as an art therapist requires that students acquire a knowledge and understanding of the self, the client and of the nature of psychotherapeutic relationships as mediated through art and its processes. Linking theoretical and experiential studies with clinical experience tends to be an intellectually and emotionally demanding business for all concerned.

One of the dilemmas inherent in becoming an art therapist is that the process is as much a matter of learning about feelings as it is about acquiring theoretical knowledge and technical skills. This can, initially, be a frightening prospect and it is not unusual for the sense of anticipation and excitement felt by students at the beginning of their training to be replaced by feelings of confusion and anxiety. During training this discomfort may find expression in a number of different ways. It may, for instance, take the form of an envious attack on course tutors or place-ment supervisors for appearing to withhold ready-made solutions to the problems they are grappling with. Such feelings often originate in the hopes and expectations the student felt in relation to parents or previous teachers. Commenting on the student's expectation that the teacher fulfil the role of provider and comforter, Salzberger-Wittenberg et al. comment,

> A body of theory can of course be taught, but it would be a purely intellectual acquisition likely to delude its possessor into believing that he knows some-thing about the mind when all he has got is a tool for categorising people. This is a dangerous attitude and a far cry from understanding based on empathy. It is also totally useless if the task is to learn to appreciate the individuality of each person and to provide a relationship that gives students the opportunity to develop. (1992: 27)

By its very nature therapeutic work of the kind art therapists are engaged in is often paradoxical, and the complexities of integrating theory and practice, intimacy and distance, words and images, can come to feel intol-erable. Within the student group this may lead to a polarisation of attitudes towards theory and practice. For some students, acquiring a theoretical understanding of the work may be felt to be of paramount importance. For others quite the opposite may apply, with theory coming to be seen as a threat to spontaneity. It is largely for these reasons that central to the teaching philosophy on UK art therapy training courses is the belief that effective learning about the process of therapeutic change, and the role image making may play in promoting this, requires that students explore and share their own feelings and perceptions.

Course Structure and Organisation

All the UK art therapy training courses are run in two modes, full time over two years, or part time over three years. The taught elements of these courses follow the standard academic year and are usually run over two 15 week semesters. Clinical placements and personal therapy, however, involve a time commitment throughout the year. Although there are varia-tions in the way the art therapy training courses are organised and struc-tured, all consist of a mix of lectures, seminars, workshops, placement experience and written work.

Lectures and Seminars

The precise content of the lecture and seminar programmes often vary from course to course, and from year to year, depending upon the needs of the student group and in response to developments within the profession. In general terms, however, lectures and seminars aim to cover the following areas:

- Basic psychotherapeutic concepts concerned with establishing and maintaining the therapeutic frame and relationship.
- An overview of the theory and practice of art therapy; including the theoretical and historical background to art therapy.
- An introduction to different therapeutic approaches to working with images and work with different client groups.
- An exploration of group and institutional dynamics.
- An examination of the political and cultural contexts in which art therapy takes place.
- In line with the attention now paid to professional ethics, research and evidence based practice, these issues have also come to assume increasing importance within the curriculum (see Chapter 7).

These components of the course are supported by tutorials and assessed through the submission of written work.

In addition to attending lectures and seminars, all students are required to undertake a number of experiential units of study.

Training Groups

During the first year of the course students spend time each week in a training group working together with an experienced art therapist. The groups usually have a membership of seven or eight students and last for two or more hours. The purpose of these groups is to enable students to gain an understanding of how art may be used therapeutically, and how image making may inform group psychodynamics (Gilroy, 1995). To this end, the training groups involve:

- Self-exploration through image making.
- Learning about group interactions and the role of image making in relation to this.
- Working with unconscious processes.
- Experimenting with different ways of image making, different materials, themes and approaches. (Swan-Foster et al., 2001)

The training groups seek to combine experiential and didactic approaches to learning. That is to say, they may include instruction on group dynamics or different approaches to working with images in groups, in addition to working with more personal material. However, although personal material and inter-personal issues inevitably surface in such groups, the training group is not a substitute for personal therapy.

Workshops

At different points during the course students may also participate in art based workshops on specific themes or issues. These workshops often involve visiting art therapists and may be scheduled to last for a whole morning or afternoon.

Supervised Clinical Practice

Students are required to complete a minimum of 120 days supervised clinical practice during their training. This is intended to provide students with a continuous, in-depth experience of psychotherapeutic work with clients using image making. This element of training is of central importance to each student's learning on the course and examines their ability to learn through experience and link theory to practice. While on placement, students work closely with a supervisor who meets with them on a regular basis to discuss their work with clients. In most situations the supervisor will be a senior art therapist. Where this is not the case the supervisor will usually be a therapist who has a sound understanding of art therapy and the training requirements of the student. One of the paradoxes of supervised clinical practice is that while it offers a potentially rewarding opportunity for the trainee to reflect upon and learn from their experience, it also involves a degree of self-exposure and the revealing of perceived fears, vulnerabilities and weaknesses. At the mid-point, and again towards the end of their placement, students are required to submit a case study or clinical report based upon their work with one or more clients.

Clinical Supervision

In addition to the supervision received while on placement, students also receive group supervision provided by course staff. The purpose of these supervision groups is to complement the supervision students receive on placement and to assist them with their learning about therapeutic work. Initially the main focus of these supervision groups tends to be primarily concerned with practical matters, such as how the students find suitable clients to work with and how to establish a safe space in which to work. Over time, however, a wider perspective is adopted in order to accommodate issues, thoughts, feelings and images arising out of the placement situation as a whole, in addition to the content of particular sessions (Edwards, 1993c; 1994).

Although the supervision provided on placement, and by course staff, are intended to complement each other, there are important and necessary distinctions to be made between them:

- The first, and perhaps most obvious, distinction between the two is that the former takes place in a variety of settings.
- The second distinction to be made is that the supervision students receive while on placement is usually provided on an individual basis.
- A third distinction is that although the majority of placement supervisors are art therapists – by profession or training – not all are.
- The final, but very important distinction to be made is that while placement supervisors do have a responsibility to meet the training needs of the student their primary responsibility is to the clients the student is working with.

The quality of the relationship established between supervisors and students is a crucial factor in determining whether or not it is successful in its aim of facilitating learning. Though clearly not the only factor, it is nevertheless one that will largely determine whether or not, at the end of an art therapist's training, they are able to use art as a means of offering distinct therapeutic help to clients.

Personal Therapy

Throughout the period of training all students are also required to be in personal therapy on a minimum basis of one hour per week. Personal therapy is a mandatory part of the course, but is not assessed. The only requirement is that the student's therapist informs the course in writing at regular intervals that therapy is continuing. Students are expected to arrange and pay the full cost of their own therapy.

There are a number of reasons why personal therapy has been included as a component of psychotherapeutic training courses:

- Firstly, personal therapy offers the student an additional opportunity to learn through experience, and helps to develop his or her overall understanding of the therapeutic process.
- Secondly, personal therapy provides the student with an opportunity to recognise and address their own unresolved problems so that they are better able to cope with the stresses of working with clients without undue interference from internal conflict.
- Finally, undertaking personal therapy outside the course offers students a level of emotional support that the course itself is unable to provide.

Because the vast majority of art therapists working in the UK are employed in the public sector (i.e. in the NHS or social service establishments), finding an art therapist able to provide therapy privately can prove problematic. The membership directory published annually by the British Association of Art Therapists (BAAT, 2003) does include a list of art therapists who work privately, but the current level of provision in this area is not extensive. Consequently many students enter therapy with therapists who may have no background in art or art therapy. In these circumstances, it is generally recommended that those forms of therapy which value and are able to work with imagery, be this verbal or pictorial, and which stress the importance of interpersonal relationships are most likely to be relevant and useful.

What is an Art Therapist?

Following their training, a qualified art therapist can be expected to possess a considerable body of knowledge and experience concerned with art, the creative processes and non-verbal communication and be able to provide an environment within which patients or clients feel safe enough to articulate and explore their feelings through the medium of art. In relation to their clinical work an art therapist should have the ability to:

- Provide art therapy in keeping with the policies of the institution in which he/she is employed.
- Establish the necessary physical and psychological conditions for implementing art therapy.
- Evaluate and report on the outcomes and effectiveness of art therapy.
- Be open and flexible enough to adapt the type and style of therapy offered to a wide range of clients.
- Cope with the problems of working in a stressful environment.
- Provide information on the nature and theory of art therapy to colleagues and other professionals.
- Be aware of his/her own emotional responses to clients and be objective and sensitive in handling relationships with them.
- Be sensitive to issues of difference (racial, cultural, sexual, class, etc.) and how these may impact upon the therapeutic relationship.
- Undertake the managerial and administrative tasks for which they have responsibility.

It is this combination of skills and experience that enable art therapists to contribute in a unique way to the multi-disciplinary teams with whom they work. In the UK, the standards of proficiency required of practicing art therapists are determined and regulated by the Health Professions Council (see Chapter 7).

Thorough though the training art therapists undertake may be, it is only the beginning of a life-long process of professional development. In addition to maintaining and extending their skills as artists and therapists through further training, attending conferences, remaining up-to-date with the literature and continuing with their own image making, art therapists often acquire other specialist skills in areas related to their work. This might include the use of computers and information technology, clinical audit, research, supervision and teaching. The continuing professional development undertaken by art therapists is discussed in more detail in the following chapter.

7

PROFESSIONAL ISSUES

By the early 1960s increasing numbers of artists were able to find employment in hospitals and clinics throughout the UK. Often this employment would be on an ad hoc basis and poorly paid. Art therapists soon began to appreciate that for their terms and conditions of employment to improve, and for the profession as a whole to develop, it was necessary to have a central organisation to represent their collective interests and to whom the general public or employing authorities could refer to for advice and information.

The British Association of Art Therapists

In 1964 the British Association of Art Therapists (BAAT) was formed and in 1966 the association held its first AGM. To paraphrase Waller, the aims of the Association at the time of its formation were:

- To promote the use of art and other creative activities as a form of therapy.
- To promote the interests of its members.
- To represent ideas concerning art therapy to the general public and other interested bodies.
- To co-operate with other organisations, 'in pursuit of the objects of the Association'.
- To encourage entry into the profession, develop training courses and establish standards of professional competence for its members. (1991: 113)

In order to achieve these aims, it was necessary for BAAT to combine the functions of a learned society, a trade union, a pressure group and a professional association; see Waller (1991), for a detailed discussion of the formation of the British Association of Art Therapists and its role in shaping the profession in the UK. During its existence BAAT has continued to focus its efforts on fulfilling these ambitions through negotiating on behalf of its members on matters such as pay and conditions of employment, through close links with the trade union movement. In addition, the Association has developed nationally recognised criteria for training and standards of professional practice, organised conferences, publishes a bi-annual journal (*Inscape*) and a newsletter and answers enquiries from the general public.[1] As at March, 2004, the total membership of BAAT is 1,435.

In 1982, due largely to work conducted by the British Association of Art Therapists, the profession was formally recognised by the Department of Health and Social Security and art therapists were, for the first time, offered salaries and conditions of employment comparable to other allied health professionals such as occupational therapists. In 1984 BAAT published its 'Principles of Professional Practice for Art Therapists' (BAAT, 1984) and in 1986 it published the first national register of qualified art therapists working in the UK. This register of members, since re-titled the Membership Directory, continues to be published on an annual basis (BAAT, 2003). In 1990 the then National Joint Council for Local Authorities formally recognised the professional qualifications of art therapists, effectively paving the way for the recognition of art therapists working in social and community services as professionals.

The executive body of BAAT, which has responsibility for managing the Associations business, is the Council. The Council consists of four officers (Chair, Vice-Chair, Honorary Secretary and Honorary Treasurer) and elected members. All members of BAAT Council are elected at the Associations AGM and serve for a fixed period of office. Representatives for the Associations working parties and sub-groups also attend Council meetings. These working parties and sub-groups have responsibility for developing art therapy in a broad range of areas; including, working with older people, clients with autistic spectrum disorders, art therapy in education and learning disability. The Art Therapy, Race and Culture (ARC) sub-group, for example, gathers information about issues related to race and culture within art therapy. The aim being to develop awareness regarding equal opportunities issues, improve training and practice and support art therapists who work across cultural and racial boundaries.

In order to support the work of art therapists at a local level the British Association of Art Therapists has 21 Regional Groups spread throughout the UK. There are also two further groups covering the European Union and the rest of the world. The Regional Groups meet with varying frequency. In addition to providing a forum for discussion and the dissemination of information, they also sponsor activities as diverse as hosting national conferences through to presentations and workshops on themes or issues of particular interest to practicing art therapists.

As a result of its work and achievements, BAAT has emerged as the official voice of art therapy in the UK. Although conflicts have emerged within the Association from time to time over such matters as the criteria for membership, training standards and, as noted in Chapter 1, the use of the title art psychotherapist, it has nevertheless provided a necessary forum for debating and reconciling potential splits and divisions. This containing function has proved invaluable in helping to facilitate the emergence of art therapy as an independent profession in the UK.

State Registration

In 1997, following a long campaign, art therapists attained state registration when the Professions Supplementary to Medicine Act of 1960 was extended to include Art, Drama and Music Therapists. By joining the Council for Professions Supplementary to Medicine art therapy became one of the first 'wholly psychotherapeutic' professions to be covered by the Act (Waller, 1999: 110). In addition to affording formal recognition by the state through protecting the professions title, registration also offers greater protection to the public by ensuring that art therapists are appropriately trained and able to practice competently. In effect, state registration defines the nature and extent of the work undertaken by art therapists and regulates their interactions with clients and other health professionals.

In April 2002, the Health Professions Council (HPC) replaced CPSM as the body responsible for the registration of art therapists. As Waller (1999: 110) comments, by replacing the unpopular title 'supplementary to medicine', the creation of the HPC also gives 'a more up-to-date impression of the professions represented by CPSM'. For many art therapists in the UK this change has been particularly welcome because it helps free the profession from its long, and often unhelpful, association with the 'medical model' of psychiatry. The HPC is an independent, UK-wide regulatory body responsible for setting and maintaining standards of professional training, performance and conduct of the 12 healthcare professions that it regulates. In addition to arts therapists (i.e. art, music and drama therapists) these currently include occupational therapists, physiotherapists and speech and language therapists. All art therapists who have successfully completed a postgraduate training approved by the HPC are automatically eligible for registration. The HPC also has responsibility for checking applications to join the register made by art therapists who trained outside the UK. Once registered, State Registered Art Therapists are required to retain their names on the register, by paying a retention fee. In July 2003 registration with the HPC became a two-yearly (biennial) process and registrants are required to state that they have continued to meet the required standards of conduct, proficiency and ethics (Health Professions Council, 2003). Depending on personal preference, a State Registered Arts Therapist may be identified by the title SRAsTh (A) or SRAT (A); the initial in brackets indicating the particular modality of the therapist (e.g. Art,

Drama or Music). As at February, 2004, 2,031 Art Therapists are registered by the HPC.

Codes of Ethics and Principles of Professional Practice

An important aspect of the regulatory function of BAAT and other art therapy associations is to ensure that the work practicing art therapists undertake is professionally and ethically sound. Registered art therapists are expected to uphold the interests of clients at all times and not to discriminate against them on such grounds as race, class, gender, age or sexual orientation. The main means of achieving this has been through the introduction and development of the ethical and professional codes that inform and regulate the clinical practice in the UK and elsewhere in the world.[2]

The purpose of a code of ethics is to publicly articulate agreed standards of conduct, professional judgement and integrity. In the Statement of Conduct published by the Arts Therapists Board Disciplinary Committee of CPSM, for instance, it is stated that,

> An AsT [Registered Arts Therapist] should confine him/herself to practise in those fields in which he/she has received appropriate and approved education, training experience and process supervision and to abide by the scope of practice laid down in the relevant professional body's Code of Ethics. (CPSM, 2000: 4)

The publication of BAAT's 'Principles of Professional Practice for Art Therapists' (PPP) (BAAT, 1984), and later the 'Code of Ethics and Principles of Professional Practice for Art Therapists' (BAAT, 1994) marked important stages in the professional development of art therapy in the UK. The publication of the PPP document, for example, represented the first attempt to bring together much of the collective knowledge and experience of art therapists working in Britain in order to offer a set of agreed guidelines for the practice of art therapy. These guidelines covered such matters as confidentiality, record keeping, exhibitions and caseloads. In addition to seeking to protect clients, the PPP also sought to establish standards for the conditions of employment of art therapists. In the mid-1990s, as art therapy moved closer to becoming a state registered profession, the PPP were revised and a code of ethics for art therapists was formulated. The distinction to be drawn between professional principles and a code of ethics is that the former represents a collection of values and standards intended to inform the work art therapists undertake, whereas the latter provides a set of rules for conduct. At the present time BAAT's Code of Ethics and Principles of Professional Practice for Art Therapists is undergoing further revision to bring it into line with recent legislation such as the Race Relations (Amendment) Act 2000, the Human Rights Act 1998, the Data Protection Act 1998 and the Disability Discrimination Act 1995.

Ethical Dilemmas

By its very nature, the kind of work undertaken by art therapists presents practitioners with professional and ethical dilemmas of one kind or another. Moreover, because art therapy usually results in the production of a material record of the therapeutic process in the form of paintings, drawings or three-dimensional objects, these dilemmas are often unique to the profession. The issue of client confidentiality raises a number of problematic issues for art therapists in relation to this (Edwards, 1993a; Kessler, 1993; Maclagan, 1993; Moon, 2000). Confidentiality is a vital aspect of all therapeutic relationships and a necessary prerequisite for establishing conditions of trust and safety. Clients are, quite rightly, concerned to protect their privacy and ensure that what they say or express through their artwork will not be detrimental to their interests. The creation of images suggestive of sexual abuse may, for example, give rise to ethical dilemmas in relation to striking a sound balance between maintaining the integrity of the therapeutic relationship and the responsibility to share information with colleagues (BAAT, 1992b). Although such dilemmas are not uncommon, many of the ethical conflicts and issues facing art therapists are more mundane, but no less problematic, as the following example illustrates.

'Chris'

Chris, a thirty-five-year-old man, was referred for art therapy because he was becoming increasingly anxious and withdrawn. Wherever possible he avoided contact with other people. Although he felt his social isolation was necessary in order to avoid feeling anxious in the company of other people, he also felt imprisoned by this. To help him manage his anxiety, Chris's psychiatrist had prescribed him a mild tranquilliser in addition to referring him for art therapy.

At the beginning of art therapy sessions Chris occasionally appeared distracted, but apart from this quickly settled down to using them to make images. After a few weeks a noticeable feature of his images was that they began to include references to 'drug culture'. The central motif of one of his images, for instance, was a leaf, that, on closer inspection, seemed to be unmistakably a cannabis leaf. When asked about its significance Chris confided, somewhat reluctantly, that smoking cannabis played an important role in his life. He said he had been smoking cannabis regularly for at least the past ten years, and possibly longer. Chris said it helped him relax, unlike alcohol, which made him feel aggressive, depressed or physically sick. Having told me this, Chris also revealed that he had stopped taking the medication his psychiatrist prescribed. Chris said he hadn't told his psychiatrist this yet, but would do so when the time felt right.

This situation presented a number of ethical dilemmas. Should the psychiatrist be informed, even though the client had indicated that he would prefer to do this himself? Should the police be informed about Chris's activities? Indeed, was it necessary to do anything? Faced with such a situation, the question 'What is the correct thing to do?' may be a very difficult one to resolve to the satisfaction of all concerned. Not informing the psychiatrist that Chris had discontinued his medication might be considered unethical in so far as non-disclosure could be perceived as failure to preserve the therapeutic interests of the client. It could also be considered unprofessional in that it might undermine a good working relationship with a colleague. On the other hand disclosing this information might well threaten the therapeutic relationship established with Chris.

In this particular case, I did not inform the psychiatrist directly that Chris had stopped taking his medication, but did impress upon him the importance of doing so himself. I did, however, make a note of what Chris had told me in his case file. I also felt it was important to begin exploring with Chris his reasons for smoking cannabis. This was particularly important as whatever legal or health issues smoking cannabis might raise he seemed to be using the drug to avoid difficult feelings.

Even the most detailed codes of ethics are unable to resolve every possible ethical or professional dilemma an art therapist may face, and other art therapists might well have dealt with the situation described above in another way. What is required is that following the principles outlined in the ethical and professional codes to which they subscribe, art therapists exercise informed, sound and responsible judgement to the benefit of the clients they seek to help.

Supervision

The expectation that all art therapists be seen to be practicing competently and professionally has resulted in increasing attention being paid to the nature and quality of the supervision they provide or receive (see BAAT, 2002; Edwards, 1994, Feinberg, 1993 and Wilson et al., 1984).

Nowadays, supervision is regarded as an essential element in the training and continuing education of all mental health professionals, including art therapists. In the British Association of Art Therapists Code of Ethics it is stated that, 'Art Therapists should monitor their own professional competence through regular supervision, either within the work place or by private arrangement' (BAAT, 1994).

One problem we immediately face when discussing the supervision of art therapists concerns what the term 'supervision' actually means. Numerous definitions exist and the term is open to widely differing interpretations. Nevertheless, supervision is generally understood to refer to the process by which the therapist receives support and guidance in order to ensure the needs of the client are recognised and responded to appropriately. Two separate, but often overlapping, forms of supervision may be identified in relation to this, 'clinical' supervision and 'managerial' supervision (BAAT, 2002). The kind of functions encompassed by the former might include looking at and discussing images made by a particular client as well as examining the client therapist relationship and the ways in which this might promote or inhibit therapeutic change. The latter might include reviewing the art therapist's work within the wider context of the employing organisation as a whole. To this end supervision is usually concerned with supporting, developing and overseeing art therapists in their therapeutic role. As Case and Dalley state,

> Supervision of the work in art therapy is considered essential for all practitioners. After graduation and during the first years of work, the art therapist needs not only support and guidance but also extensive understanding of the dynamics of the complex relationships that develop in the clinical work. Even after years of experience most art therapists should have a regular supervision session built into their working programme as, continually, new light can be placed on the working practice with objective insights and new understandings of the work. (1992: 167)

Although a broad consensus now exists within the profession regarding the importance of supervision, notable differences exist concerning the means by which the generally agreed aims of supervision might best be accomplished. The extent to which supervision is actually able to help art therapists learn, develop and provide a safe service to clients will be determined by a number of factors. These include:

- The professional background and theoretical orientation of the supervisor. While many art therapists are supervised by more experienced members of the profession, not all are. In its recently published guidelines for the supervision of State Registered Art Therapists, the advice offered by the British Association of Art Therapists is that they 'should not be supervised by anyone who does not themselves possess a psychodynamic training or whose training is not compatible (in that they do not address transference and counter transference issues) or who has not undergone supervision themselves' (BAAT, 2002).

- The quality of the working relationship established between the supervisor and supervisee is another factor likely to influence the outcome of supervision. It is therefore essential that the supervisor values and has a commitment to supervision, a sound understanding of art therapy and that they are able to provide helpful feedback in a clear, non-judgemental way. It is also important that the supervision provided is creative, confidential, and regular, affords opportunities for reflection and is sufficiently flexible to meet the art therapist's needs at different stages of their career.
- The way in which supervision is organised can also play a crucial role in determining its usefulness. Supervision may, for example, be provided individually or in a group. Some supervisors require their supervisee's to bring detailed notes as well as images to sessions, while others prefer a less structured, more spontaneous approach (Maclagan, 1997).
- Finally, another important variable likely to influence supervision concerns the personalities of the individuals involved, along with such factors as their gender, age or race (Calish, 1998).

In practice, the supervision process involves a combination of emotional support and experiential learning; along with much in between. Any given supervision session may, therefore, encompass both a theoretical discussion concerning an aspect of clinical practice, and an exploration of thoughts and feelings arising in response to clients and their images. Essentially, the supervisors task is to create a space for thinking, feeling and reflection; 'space for a certain degree of reverie in which peripheral thoughts, feelings and fantasies in relation to the patient can be brought into awareness and examined' (Mollon, 1989: 120). If the supervisor is able to help create such a space, the supervisory relationship may then become one in which the art therapist is free to play and imagine. The familiarity art therapists have with image making and the creative process can be of considerable help in enabling them to make use of supervision in this way. This would seem to be particularly so if the art therapist makes images as part of supervision (Lett, 1995). Making images an integral part of the supervision process, either immediately after a session or in supervision, can prove to be an especially fruitful way of furthering the art therapist's understanding of, as well as containing and recollecting, what happens in art therapy (Henzell, 1997a).

'John'

Some years ago I was supervising a male art therapist, John, who was very distressed about an incident that had happened in his work with a female client. After establishing what John believed to be a good working relationship with his client, quite unexpectedly from his point of view, she had angrily accused him of all manner of misdemeanors amounting to professional misconduct. Recounting the experience in supervision, he did so in such a way as to leave me in no doubt as to how he felt. John described it as like being hit by an Exocet missile. He felt he had no warning of the attack, his radar had let him down (that is to say, I had let him down) and the experience had been destructive.

It was only after it had proved possible to allay John's distress suffi- ciently to be able to think creatively about what had happened that the significance of his client's attack began to unfold. John's image of being subject to an attack from an Exocet missile was crucial in this. Exocet missiles, we should perhaps remind ourselves, are not only phallic in shape, but are intended to cause internal rather than exter- nal damage. What transpired was that unbeknown to him, or indeed anyone else involved at the time, John's client had been sexually abused as a child and was re-experiencing her feelings about this in art therapy. In abusing him, the client had let John know, in the only way she could, how she felt, not only about him, but about herself too. Arriving at a better understanding of the meaning of his client's attack enabled the therapy to continue and develop from a point at which it may well have broken down, and encouraged John to be more trusting of his own impressions and feelings as they arose in his work with clients.

Continuing Professional Development

It has long been accepted that successfully obtaining a professional quali- fication marks the beginning, not the end, of an art therapist's learning. Much knowledge and experience may yet need to be acquired to effect the transition from novice to expert. More experienced art therapists also have a professional and ethical responsibility to remain up-to-date with devel- opments in the field. Art therapists practicing today regularly engage in some form of post-registration education. This may be in the form of further training, attending conferences, short courses or workshops, or through self-directed learning; including, writing for publication, research and by continuing to develop their own art work. Art therapists have not, however, necessarily documented this activity, or reflected upon their learning in a systematic or structured way. Because of the emphasis increasingly placed on maintaining and developing clinical skills and expertise, particularly but not exclusively within the NHS, art therapists are now required to engage in what is referred to as Continuing Professional Development (CPD) (Alsop, 2000). CPD involves more than simply listing courses or workshops the art therapist may have attended. The expectation is that art therapists will both record *and* reflect upon what was learned or reconfirmed through their CPD activity. At the present time the British Association of Art Therapists recommends that art therapists record their CPD 'within the categories of "Clinical", "Managerial/ BAAT", "Academic" and "Creative"' (Cody, 2001: 10).

As CPD has become increasingly formalised and linked to maintaining professional standards and the protection of the public, it has become an important topic within art therapy in the UK. One reason for this is that the Department of Health has funded a large-scale project aimed at developing an outcomes-based approach to demonstrating the competence of allied health professionals, including art therapists, through CPD. As such CPD has come to represent a form of quality assurance. That is to say, it provides a means by which art therapists can be seen to demonstrate a commitment to developing and maintaining high standards of clinical practice in order to ensure the protection of the public. Although the link between clinical competence and CPD is difficult to define and validate, it nevertheless seems likely that in the future the re-registration of art therapists will require that practitioners demonstrate a commitment to their continuing professional development. Art therapists seeking re-accreditation in the USA are already required to do this (see Chapter 8). Exactly what CPD requirements will be introduced for art therapists working in the UK has yet to be determined.

Art Therapy Research

Research into the use of art for diagnostic purposes has played a significant role in the development of art therapy. The extensive literature generated by these enquiries into the relationship between art and mental health is extensive, although much of it is of questionable value either to art therapists or those affected by mental health problems (Thomas and Jolly, 1998). Anastasi and Foley (1944: 169), in an early review of the artwork produced by psychiatric patients, comment, 'Relatively little of a conclusive nature can ... be gleaned from the voluminous literature in this field, owing to inadequate control of experimental conditions, and to the excessive theoretical speculation which frequently obscures the data'. This observation is endorsed by Hacking (1999) in her review of the literature on the evidence of pathological characteristics in the artwork of adult psychiatric patients published over the preceding 20 years.

Nevertheless, attempts have been made, particularly by art therapists in the USA, to develop reliable assessment procedures or 'projective tests' using various forms of image making in the search for recurring themes, colours, motifs and symbols (so-called 'graphic indicators') deemed to be indicative of psychological distress (Neale and Rosal, 1993). Thus, for example, inclement weather (rain, snow, hail and/or wind) depicted in children's drawings as disproportionate and/or excessive in size, might be judged to represent an external threat, possibly of physical abuse

(Manning, 1987). Art therapists in the USA employ a wide variety of assessment tools in their clinical work and research. In addition to using well known tests such as the House-Tree-Person Test (Buck, 1992) and the Kinetic Family Drawing Test (Burns and Kaufman, 1972), these include the Diagnostic Drawing Series (DDS), the Levick Emotional and Cognitive Art Therapy Assessment (LECATA) and the Mandala Assessment Research Instrument (MARI)® Card Test©.[3] This approach is influenced by the work of such figures as Florence Goodenough (1975), Karen Machover (1949) and Emanuel Hammer (1958) who pioneered the use of drawing as a means of assessing IQ and personality development based on the belief that images directly reflect a person's sense of self, current emotional state or relationship to the external world.

Art Therapy Research in the UK

In the UK, art therapists have generally steered clear of using such image based assessment tools. Traditionally, they have also tended to eschew the kind of statistically based research methodologies employed to substantiate them. This reticence extends to evaluative research into the processes and outcomes of art therapy (Edwards, 1987). There appear to be a number of reasons for this. These include a lack of familiarity and experience with 'scientific' research methodologies, the lack of funding and support available to art therapists wishing to conduct research of any kind, and a lack of interest in research outcomes; especially those which appear to have little connection or relevance to actual clinical work (Edwards, 1993b). Moreover, the particular skills necessary to conduct research in art therapy have traditionally been perceived as being 'more appropriate to advanced training once the art therapist has gained in practical knowledge and experience' (Gilroy, 1992: 234). As a result research skills are usually acquired by art therapists following training rather than during it, although this is now changing. This is in marked contrast to the situation in the USA where basic research methods form an integral part of the curriculum. As a consequence, art therapy research in the UK is in its early stages, whereas in North America, largely for pragmatic and cultural reasons, it is relatively well established (see, for example, McNiff, 1987, 2000 and Wadeson, 1992).

This is not, however, to imply that art therapists in the UK regard research as unimportant. Art therapists do recognise that practice based research has become vitally important, and for a number of reasons:

- It might help art therapists acquire and share clinically relevant knowledge and experience.
- It offers art therapists, employers and clients an opportunity to critically assess developments within the profession.

- Research may also help clarify 'the appropriateness of one model of work compared to another with a particular client group' (Gilroy and Lee, 1995: 8).
- Research can help ensure clinical accountability and efficacy.

Research in art therapy is also necessary because,

> Those fighting for accessible, efficient, effective, user-friendly services need all the friends they can get. Psychotherapy research is one ... it is a corrective to scepticism about cost-effectiveness, to the belief that psychotherapeutic models are inapplicable to severe problems; it challenges blind allegiance to one model or the idea that anyone can do it. (Parry, 1997: 12)

Where art therapists have undertaken research, they have, as Gilroy and Lee (1995: 7) note, usually 'preferred "softer" research methodologies and have neither used the quantitative methodologies nor addressed the outcomes of their work'. See Gilroy, 1992; Gilroy and Lee, 1995; Payne, 1993 for helpful discussions of the range of approaches to research employed by arts therapists in the UK.[4]

The view that research in art therapy is not best served by modes of enquiry derived from the physical sciences has been highly influential within the profession in the UK (M. Edwards, 1981; Henzell, 1995; Maclagan, 1999). Though debates concerning the appropriateness or validity of competing research paradigms and methodologies continue, in the current economic and political climate the importance of research to art therapy cannot be underestimated. It is no longer the case that art therapists can expect, as did earlier generations, that their conviction that art therapy works will be taken simply on trust. As Gilroy (1996: 53) argues, art therapists have to evaluate their work both 'in order to enhance our professional credibility as well as to preserve and create jobs'.

Evidence Based Practice

Over the past decade, largely driven by economic, political and ethical pressures, questions regarding the provision of reliable evidence of clinical outcomes and effectiveness have become a subject of growing concern in all areas of health care. In response to these concerns increasing emphasis has been placed on the need to conduct research that conforms to the requirements of evidence-based medicine (EBM) and/or evidence based practice (EBP); EBP being 'the conscientious, explicit and judicious use of current best evidence in making decisions about the care of individuals' (Sackett et al., 1996, in Goss and Rose, 2002: 147). EBP has assumed importance for art therapists because the NHS has introduced an evidence based National Service Framework for all areas of health care; including mental health (Department of Health, 1999).

The Department of Health has also recently published guidelines on treatment choice in the psychological therapies (Department of Health, 2001).[5] The aim of these guidelines, which include references to the Arts Therapies, is to help ensure clients receive the appropriate form of psychological therapy. Information contributing to the evidence base supporting the provision of health care are collated and disseminated by a number of organisations, including the National Institute for Clinical Excellence (NICE), the Cochrane Collaboration and the NHS Centre for Reviews and Dissemination based at the University of York. The NHS Centre for Reviews and Dissemination database currently carries only one systematic review of a research paper on the effectiveness of art therapy (Reynolds et al., 2000).[6]

Issues concerning the kind and quality of evidence that might be considered valid when judged by the criteria of evidence based practice are undeniably problematic for art therapists. Not least because, as Gilroy (1996: 53) remarks, 'There is very little published art therapy research available in this country and I doubt very much whether what is available would satisfy the "rules of evidence" and principles of EBM/EBP'. In theory, a variety of approaches to research may contribute to the evidence base for art therapy. In practice, however, there is a clearly defined hierarchy of evidence with the systematic comparison (meta-analysis) of randomised controlled trials (RCT's) at the peak and professional consensus at the bottom. Randomised controlled trials are important to those who provide or use services because they explicitly ask questions about the comparative benefits of two or more forms of treatment. RCT's are now widely regarded as providing the best source of evidence for the efficacy of various forms of psychological treatment. A major drawback of the RCT when applied to psychological therapies such as art therapy, however, is that art therapists work in different ways, even with the same client population. Moreover, as discussed elsewhere in this book, the term 'art therapy' means different things to different people, thus making comparisons problematic, if not in fact impossible. RCT's are also complex, expensive to run and generally require powerful institutional backing to conduct. At present, few art therapists are in a position to conduct research of this kind, although attempts have been made to do so (Jones et al., 1998; Reynolds et al., 2000; Waller, 2002).

Art therapists have responded to the need to expand the evidence base for art therapy in a variety of different ways. In one of the earliest papers to discuss art therapy research in the UK, Males (1980) outlines what she regards as the respective merits of investigation and inquiry in art therapy, including, single case studies, surveys and controlled experimental investigations. Wood (1999) identifies a number of alternative strategies for gathering evidence on art therapy practice and outcomes. These include clinical audit, collecting census information and using standardised assessment and outcome measures such as those developed by the CORE System Group (CORE System Group, 1998). Gilroy (2001: 3) suggests that, in addition to conducting RCT's and simple outcome studies, evidence could also be generated through 'systematic observational studies and other qualitative, collaborative and heuristic research'. In this context, heuristic research refers to research grounded in the personal experience of the researcher (see Moustakas, 1990). An important recent development in this direction has been the formation of the Art Therapists Practice Research Network (ATPRN), a UK-wide group of art therapists who collaborate on practice–led research and evaluation ventures.

Until such time as sufficient numbers of art therapists acquire the research skills necessary to extend the evidence base of the profession, the case study is likely to remain the most popular means of describing, evaluating and providing a theoretical account of art therapy conducted in different settings and with different client groups (see, for example, Dalley et al., 1993; Schaverien, 1992). While not without its limitations, as a method of enquiry into both the process and outcome of art therapy, the case study nevertheless has a number of strengths (Edwards, 1999; Higgins, 1993):

- Firstly, it is a method of enquiry that pays serious attention to the individuality of the client. That is, to his or her particular problems or difficulties, and to how these are communicated through their actions, words and images.
- It provides an opportunity to conduct research that is sympathetic to the actual nature of our work. It engages with, rather than avoids or limits, the richness, diversity, messiness and complexity of the therapeutic process.
- It provides an opportunity to re-examine existing theories and offer alternative explanations for what might be encountered in the clinical setting.
- Finally, the case study is a relatively inexpensive, 'user-friendly' form of research.

Whichever methods of enquiry art therapists make use of in the future, research, along with CPD and professional self-regulation, will undoubtedly play an important role in maintaining and improving the quality of care provided for those with mental health and other problems.

Notes

1. *Inscape*, the journal of the British Association of Art Therapists, was founded in 1969. The journal took its title from the term originally conceived by the poet Gerard Manley Hopkins in the mid-1860s (Lanham, 2002). Hopkins used the word 'inscape' to describe the distinctive nature of a form; that which 'constitutes the rich and revealing "one-ness" of a natural object' (Gardner, 1985: xx).

2. Examples of codes of ethics regulating the conduct of art therapists in the USA and Canada can be found at www.arttherapy.org/EthicsDocuments.htm (American Art Therapy Association), www.arttherapy.bc.ca/code_of_ethics.html

(British Colombia Art Therapy Association) and www.oata.icomm.ca/the_oata. htm#why (Ontario Art Therapy Association).

3. Further details about these tests can be found on the AATA website at www.arttherapy.org/research/assessments.htm

4. See also McLeod (1995) and Higgins (1996) for useful introductions to the range of research methods used in counselling and other forms of psychotherapy.

5. Copies of this document can be downloaded from the Department of Health website at www.doh.gov.uk/mentalhealth/treatmentguideline/index.htm

6. This review (DARE abstract 20015001) employs a set of quality criteria and is available to read online at http://agatha.york.ac.uk/online/dare/20015001.htm A Cochrane review of the effects of art therapy as an adjunctive treatment for schizophrenia compared with standard care and other psychosocial interventions can be found at www.update-software.com/abstracts/AB003728.htm

8

An International Perspective

Due to a range of historical, cultural, economic and political factors, the practice and training of art therapists worldwide is extremely varied. As a result, art therapy is more securely established in some countries than in others. This concluding chapter examines some of the reasons for this diversity and discusses its consequences for art therapists and those they seek to help.

Art Therapy in Europe

The most extensive discussion of the development of art therapy in Europe found in the art therapy literature is that provided by Waller (1998). It is clear from Waller's book that there is considerable variation with respect to training, practice and the degree of professional development of art therapy on mainland Europe. This assessment is supported by other authors; including Gilroy and Hanna (1998), Herrmann (2000), Robinson (1992) and Vasarhelyi (1992). Although art therapy in Europe shares similar roots to the profession in the UK, as is the case elsewhere in the world, it has also been shaped by the many and varied educational, institutional and cultural contexts in which it has emerged. As a consequence, the profession has reached different levels of recognition, development and regulation. In some European countries, like Eire and Italy, art therapy is in the process of becoming an autonomous profession. In others, such as Hungary and Switzerland, the practice of art therapy remains largely subsumed within that of larger professional groups, particularly psychotherapy and psychiatry. In those European countries where art therapy is established, this has largely been achieved as a result of international co-operation between training institutes (Cagnoletta, 1990; Waller, 1992, 1998) or due to the influence of art therapists trained in the UK or USA returning home to their country of origin (Horgan, 1992). It is particularly ironic that in countries such as Austria, France, Germany and Switzerland, each of which has played such a significant role in the development of the arts and psychotherapy, art therapy has yet to fully establish itself.

Art Therapy Training in Europe

Art therapy training courses are run in most European countries, including Germany, France, Switzerland, Finland, the Netherlands and Italy. However, unlike the situation in the UK, where over 90 per cent of students entering training have a background in the visual arts, in much of Europe the position is very different. Students on art therapy training courses on the continent tend to belong to medical or paramedical professions and often have limited practical art experience (Waller, 1998). The attitudes of trainees towards mental health care and the therapeutic application of art tend, therefore, to be significantly different to their counterparts in the UK. Their understanding of art may also be very different. This may, in part, be due to the kind of art education art therapists in the UK have traditionally received.

> Although art education varied greatly in the level at which it was taught in the UK, painting as self-expression was usually found in nursery and primary schools, and art was taught as a practical subject involving materials and methods. In many parts of Europe, including Eastern Europe, art in the curriculum meant art history, or the study of classical forms. Practical art work was carried out, if at all, in after-school classes. (Waller, 1998: 54)

Reflecting on her experiences training art therapists in Hungary, Vasarhelyi writes,

> The term 'art' was even more ambiguous than it is in English. It carried not only the usual burden of aesthetic values attached to it – a misunderstanding we often encounter as Art Therapists – but was also a much too general and imprecise word. Art in Hungarian means any form of art ... It therefore opens up another source of confusion concerning identity by suggesting that it is a kind of 'creative therapy'. After careful consideration, I felt the term, 'Visual Psychotherapy', would express most clearly the essence of a therapy where the visual image is a direct reflection of internal, unconscious processes, untainted by external attributes such as skill or conformity to socially acceptable aesthetic criteria. (1992: 26)

This has often resulted in art therapy being seen as a technique or skill to be added to those already possessed by the psychiatrist, psychologist or nurse, rather than a distinct therapeutic modality. With respect to art therapy training in Germany, Herrmann notes,

> Training has been established academically into training schemes of other professions as an option for specialisation. These are mainly remedial education and educational sciences at university and polytechnic level. Also, there are postgraduate course offered by academies of fine art (Munich), as well as private training institutes (Hanover, Hamburg, Munich). (2000: 19)

Other notable differences between art therapy training in Europe and the UK concern the length of training, the academic level at which it is offered, along with differences in content. Some training courses combine the use of different art forms, while other programmes do not involve students undertaking supervised clinical placements or personal therapy.

In addition to the development of partnerships between training institutions in the UK and USA and those in countries where art therapy is not yet fully established or regulated, an important step towards bringing some cohesion to art therapy training in Europe was the founding, in 1991, of the European Consortium for Arts Therapy Education (ECArTE). ECArTE is an association of universities and higher education institutions that currently comprises 30 member institutions from ten European countries. ECArTE's primary purpose is to represent and encourage the development of the arts therapies at a European level, particularly those courses offering nationally validated and professionally recognised trainings. The work of ECArTE includes creating stronger European links through the exchange of staff and students; promoting research into methods of arts therapies practice within Europe; promoting the recognition of qualifications in the Arts Therapies at a European level and offering opportunities for professional communication via its international conferences. The 6th conference in Luxembourg 2001 attracted participants from 26 countries from all over the world.[1]

Professional Art Therapy Associations in Europe

One effect of the diversity of art therapy practice across Europe is that it has prevented, as Gilroy and Hanna (1998: 257) observe, 'the formation of strong professional associations' resulting in a lack of recognition for art therapy in some countries. Italy, for example, has one national art therapy association (Art Therapy Italiana) founded in 1982 by three US trained art therapists, although art therapy is not yet 'a recognised discipline or profession' (Waller, 1992: 12). Switzerland has two art therapy associations. One of these, the *Association Romande Arts et Therapies* (AREAT) is for French speakers, the other, longer established organisation, is the *Schweizerische Fachverband fuer Gestaltenderpsychotherapie und Kunsttherapie* (SFGK), which was founded in 1985. The membership of AREAT consists mainly of graduates from the training programme in Lausanne, which takes artists, teachers and health care professionals as trainees. The SFGK, by contrast, consists 'mostly of psychiatrists using art in their practices' (Robinson, 1992: 7). The situation in Switzerland is further complicated by the differences in approach to art therapy adopted by those who practice 'Maltherapie' (from 'malen' the German word for 'to paint') and those who practice 'Kunsttherapie' (from 'Kunst', the German word for art). The latter approach, according to Robinson (1992), places greater emphasis on the interpretation of images, whereas the former emphasises self-expression. These differences in approach to art therapy, along with an evident lack of co-operation between the various groups using art as part of their practice, appears to have resulted in the profession remaining unrecognised and largely subsumed under other professions (see also Stitelmann, 1998).

Herrmann (2000: 19) describes a similar picture in Germany where 'the federal psychotherapy law, passed in 1997, excludes art and music therapy on the grounds of insufficiently regulated training and the poorly developed images of the profession'. In effect, this has limited the employment opportunities for art therapists because health insurance companies will only pay for therapy, primarily psychoanalysis and behaviour therapy, provided by those professions that have access to legal registration, 'These professions are normally restricted to medical doctors and psychologists' (Dannecker in Waller, 1998: 108). This is despite the fact that art therapy is widely practiced, that Germany has 11 professional associations and hosts some 30 undergraduate and postgraduate art therapy training courses! (Herrmann, 2000)

Elsewhere in Europe the professional organisation of art therapy remains similarly fragmented, although examples of professional associations working together across disciplines and across national borders are to be found. Ireland has two art therapy associations, the Northern Ireland Group for Art as Therapy (NIGAT) and the Dublin based Irish Association of Creative Arts Therapists (IACAT), both of which seek to work collaboratively to advance the arts therapies professions in Ireland (Horgan, 1992, 1998). The distinguished art therapist Rita Simon founded NIGAT in 1976. IACAT, which changed its name from the Irish Association of Drama, Art and Music Therapists to its present one in 1998, was founded in 1992 by a group of arts therapists who had trained abroad and were in the process of establishing their professions in Ireland.

Despite such positive developments, the fragmentation of art therapy in Europe has undoubtedly inhibited its growth as an autonomous profession. It also, as Waller (1998) notes, presents art therapy with numerous challenges regarding the free movement of professionals within the European Union as outlined in EU Directive 89/48.

> Given the kind of assessment of an applicant's potential for working as an art therapist that is going to be required under the Directive, it is necessary to be precise about the nature and level of the work to be undertaken. In a new profession such as art therapy, the position is far from clear. (1998: 60)

Until such time as there is wider agreement within Europe on what art therapy is and how art therapists should be trained, organised and regulated, the free movement of professionals across the continent is unlikely to be achieved. It is doubtful whether this 'harmonisation' can be achieved without the formation of professional art therapy associations able to 'contain philosophical and individual difference' while attracting a 'critical mass of working members' (Gilroy and Hanna, 1998: 272).

Art Therapy in the USA

The key figure in advancing the development of art therapy in the United States was undoubtedly Margaret Naumberg. Although others had been employed as art therapists before her, 'Naumberg was the first to delineate art therapy as a separate profession and a distinct form of psychotherapy' (Junge and Asawa, 1994: 22).[2] Naumberg's professional background was in psychology and education and she drew upon this to create what would become art therapy. In 1914 Naumburg founded the Children's School, later renamed the Walden School. Influenced by progressive educational methods such as those promoted by Franz Cizek in Vienna and her elder sister Florence Cane, at the Walden School Naumberg put into practice her belief that teaching which cultivated spontaneity and self-directed learning were preferable to more traditional approaches. In 1920, Naumburg invited her sister to teach at the Walden School after she had criticised the way that art was being taught there. At that time, the use of feelings as a source for creativity was not popular among art teachers and most art teaching was directed towards instructing children on how to draw realistically. In contrast to this, the approach to art teaching Florence Cane advocated often used scribbling and free association with the aim of tapping into the unconscious mind of the child and liberating their imagination.[3]

Naumberg's educational methods were also influenced by psychoanalysis. Naumberg had been in therapy with Dr Beatrice Hinkle, a Jungian, and later in life began a personal analysis with Dr A.A. Brill, a leading Freudian. From 1930 onwards, Naumberg moved away from progressive education and increasingly concerned herself with developing art therapy. Between 1941 and 1947 she undertook research into the therapeutic use of art at the New York Psychiatric Institute. Naumberg's first two books, *Studies of the 'Free' Art Expression of Behavior Problem Children and Adolescents as a Means of Diagnosis and Therapy* (1947) and *Schizophrenic Art: Its meaning in psychotherapy* (1950) stemmed from this research. In 1953 Naumburg published Psychoneurotic Art and in 1966 she published Dynamically Oriented Art Therapy. Dynamically oriented art therapy was based on,

> The recognition that Man's fundamental thoughts and feelings are derived from the unconscious and often reach expression in images rather than words. By means of pictorial projection, art therapy encourages a method of symbolic communication between patient and therapist. (Naumberg, 1966: 1)

Naumberg's approach to art therapy emphasised the value of using art as a means of spontaneously releasing the power of the unconscious. This, she argued, had the advantage of circumventing the limitations of verbal speech and evading self-censorship. However, although her way of working was largely based on Freudian theory, and acknowledged the importance of the relationship between patient and therapist, it also differed from classical psychoanalytic technique in a number of significant ways. Naumberg's patients were encouraged to adopt a more active, less dependent, position within the therapeutic relationship and to offer their own interpretations of the images they produced. Naumberg's focus on integrating art and psychotherapy helped establish one pole of the continuum along which art therapy subsequently developed, both in the USA and elsewhere.

A decade or so later, the opposite pole on this continuum found its chief advocate in the work of Edith Kramer, who emphasised the healing potential of the art process itself. Kramer's approach to art therapy was primarily influenced by ideas concerning psychoanalytically informed education and child analysis. Ideas Kramer first became aware of in Vienna and Prague prior to emigrating to the USA in 1938 and which she later drew upon when working as an art therapist at Wiltwyck, a residential school for disturbed boys in New York, in 1951. Because Kramer emphasises the idea of art as therapy, rather than the use of image making within psychotherapy, it is often assumed she made little use of psychoanalytic theory. In actual fact, while Kramer and Naumberg developed approaches to art therapy that were very different, both drew extensively upon psychoanalytic theory, but in very different ways. Kramer's interests reside not so much in using art or the therapeutic relationship to bring unconscious conflicts into conscious awareness, but in drawing upon the creative process itself as a means of integrating conflicting feelings.

> Even though my therapeutic approach includes awareness of psychic processes that may remain unconscious, the therapeutic manoeuvres I am apt to employ seldom include uncovering unconscious material or the interpretation of unconscious meaning. (Kramer, 2000: 18)

For Kramer, the art therapist's primary task is to support the client/artist's ego and to utilise the intrinsic power of art in the service of psychological development. Moreover, in contrast to Naumberg who, following Freud, emphasised content rather than form, in Kramer's view the aesthetic quality of an artwork was of primary importance. As Junge and Asawa (1994: 37) comment 'the more fully realised and aesthetically pleasing the art, the more complete the sublimation, which to Kramer is the primary goal of art therapy' (see Chapter 4).

During the 1960s and 1970s art therapy in the USA developed rapidly due to a combination of factors, including the promotional efforts of Naumberg and Kramer, among others, changing attitudes to mental illness and, as in the UK, through the patronage of influential psychiatrists and psychoanalysts. An important landmark in this process was the founding, in 1961, of the *Bulletin of Art Therapy* (later renamed the *American Journal of Art Therapy*) by Elinor Ulman. This journal, the first of its kind, played a particularly significant role in the dissemination of ideas concerning art therapy by providing the emerging profession with a focus and an independent voice, both within the USA and internationally. It is difficult to determine whether the importance attached to publication by US art therapists is due to the sense of isolation engendered by geography, individual temperament or the nature of academic life in North America. Whatever the reason may be, US-based art therapists have, from the 1950s to date, made a prolific and influential contribution to the art therapy literature. Indeed until the mid-1980s almost all the books on art therapy available in the UK originated in the USA. Influential though the art therapy literature has undeniably been in furthering the development of art therapy in the USA, more important still were to be the founding of the American Art Therapy Association in 1969 and the growth of art therapy training programmes during the 1970s.

Art Therapy Training in the USA

The earliest recorded instance of an art therapy training programme in the USA was a Master's degree in art therapy offered by the University of Louisville in 1957 (Junge and Asawa, 1994: 74). Prior to this, and very much in line with the development of art therapy in the UK, art therapists usually learned their craft 'on the job'. The rapid expansion in art therapy training that took place during the 1970s may be attributed to a number of factors. These include the growing influence of the human potential movement pioneered by Abraham Maslow, Rollo May and Carl Rogers among others, along with opportunities for employment afforded by the development of community based facilities for the mentally ill. It was, however, the American Art Therapy Association's decision to make training a requirement of registration, and to set guidelines for the education of art therapists, that provided the greatest impetus for the rapid expansion of art therapy training programmes during the 1970s and 1980s. Training standards are monitored, and courses are approved, by AATA's Education and Training Board. By 1992, 32 art therapy training programmes were offered at Master's level in the US, along with many more undergraduate courses. These courses consist of a mix of taught and experiential elements, although greater emphasis is placed on the acquisition of research skills and on the use of art for assessment and diagnosis than in the UK. In 1993 the American Art Therapy Association officially determined that entry to the profession should be at Master's degree level, whereas in the UK it is that of a Post-graduate Diploma.

Many of the better known art therapists in the US have been, or continue to be, actively involved in the training and education of art therapists, including Edith Kramer (2000), Hanna Yaxa Kwiatkowska (1978), Helen Landgarten (1981), Myra Levick (the first president of the American Art Therapy Association), Cathy Malchiodi (2002), Harriet Wadeson (1994), Arthur Robbins (1994) and Elinor Ulman (2001). It is not at all surprising, therefore, to discover that art therapy training in the US is diverse and embraces a wide range of approaches and philosophies.

The American Art Therapy Association

As art therapy developed in the USA, the need to establish a distinct professional identity, develop opportunities for training and set standards for clinical practice became ever more pressing. In June 1969 the American Art

Therapy Association (AATA) was founded, despite some initial resistance to the idea. Writing in the *Bulletin of Art Therapy*, Stern and Honore argued,

> We believe that it is far too early to nationalise, and far too early to think of certification in the area of art therapy. Any such move should be preceded by further attempts to establish and disseminate a unique body of concepts and knowledge which could then be useful to other disciplines, rather than beginning with largely borrowed concepts. (1969: 95)

Some 30 years on, the American Art Therapy Association, a not-for-profit organisation, continues to set educational, professional, and ethical standards for its members and strives to educate and disseminate information about art therapy to the public. The association currently represents approximately 4,750 individuals in five membership categories (Professional, Student, Associate, Contributing, and Retired). The Association is governed and directed by an 11 member Board elected by the membership, supported by an extensive committee structure responsible for matters such as professional practice, conference organisation, education, ethics, governmental affairs and multicultural issues. Affiliate Chapters of the AATA have been established throughout the United States for the purpose of meeting and sponsoring activities that promote art therapy at a local level. AATA also publishes a newsletter and journal (*Art Therapy: Journal of the American Art Therapy Association*), along with other material relevant to the field of art therapy.

The American Art Therapy Association's decision in 1970 to establish a register of art therapists who met agreed standards was, as in the UK, widely regarded as an important step in attaining professional credibility. Though largely welcomed, registration nevertheless had its critics. Edith Kramer, for example, argued that such a step was untimely and would 'induce premature rigidity within a field that must remain flexible and open to experimentation if it is to grow and to prove its worth' (Kramer in Junge and Asawa, 1994: 127). Despite Kramer's reservations, the requirement that art therapists attain specified levels of education and experience in order to register with AATA does not appear to have resulted in either rigidity or a lack of experimentation. Indeed, the diversity of approaches encountered within art therapy in the USA is, from a UK perspective, one of its more appreciable characteristics (Byrne, 1987; Gilroy and Skaife, 1997; Woddis, 1984, 1986).

Accreditation and Licensure in the USA

The system of registering art therapists developed by AATA, though similar to that introduced in the UK by BAAT, also has a number of notable differences. These differences having been shaped mainly by the requirements of the labour market in the US. In the US, health care is not centrally funded and provided by the state, as it is in the UK through the National Health Service, but through a mix of public, charitable and for profit insurance schemes. As a consequence,

In order to work privately (and be eligible for payment through clients' medical insurance) an art therapist needs to be licensed by the legislature of the state in which they work. The requirements for licensure vary from state to state ... [but] can only be gained through training and membership of a profession which ... automatically has licensure, i.e. psychologists, social workers, counsellors or family and marital therapists ... Gaining licensure, and therefore professional and legal recognition from an individual state, is a huge issue for AATA, hence their increasing attention to art therapists' professional credentials. (Gilroy and Skaife, 1997: 60–61)

In response to this, in the early 1990s the American Art Therapy Association supported the development of a separate organisation, the Art Therapy Credentials Board, Inc. (ATCB), to register and accredit art therapists. The ATCB is a voluntary certification board that, while working closely with the AATA to further the field of art therapy, is independent of it.

Within the two-tier system overseen by the ATCB, the title 'ATR' (Art Therapist Registered) is awarded to individuals who have successfully attained the required educational and professional standards. Registered art therapists must have a Master's degree in art therapy, a solid foundation in the studio arts and therapy techniques in addition to postgraduate supervised experience. Personal therapy, though strongly recommended by most art therapy training programmes in the US is not, however, mandatory and is not, therefore, required for registration purposes. Board Certification (ATR-BC) is voluntary and granted to Registered Art Therapists who have successfully passed a national certification examination. Re-certification is awarded every five years by re-examination or by providing evidence of education, publication, presentation, exhibition or other activities demonstrating continuing professional development and competence. The title ATR-BC appears to be becoming the accepted mark of professional competence for art therapists in the US and some states are using board certification as a means to license art therapists.

One interesting effect of the pressure on art therapists to become licensed, or carry additional recognised professional credentials, has been to rekindle debates about their professional identity. As Joan Phillips, the current President of the Art Therapy Credentials Board, Inc. observes,

Many art therapists in the US seek licenses in related fields such as counsellors or as marriage and family therapists (LPC or LMFT). Art therapy degree programmes are also sometimes housed within other departments of universities that have titles that supersede art therapy. Thus some feel it is a watering down of being an art therapist if one bears the license or title of a different (and always much larger and powerful) profession. (Personal correspondence)

Currently, there are some 2,000 art therapists certified as ATR by the ATCB, and a further 1,300 who carry the title ATR-BC. This figure is growing at a rate of approximately 300 per year. These art therapists may be found practicing in a wide range of settings that include mental health, rehabilitation, medical and forensic institutions; community outreach programs; schools; nursing homes; open studios and independent practices.

Art Therapy in Canada

Art therapy in Canada dates back to the mid-1940s, when Dr Martin A. Fischer (a Toronto based psychiatrist), Irene and Selwyn Dewdney and Marie Revai began using art in their work with psychiatric patients. This was at a time before psychiatric medication began to be widely used. According to Woolf,

> In 1944 Dr Fischer offered a very agitated patient an opportunity to express himself through art by providing the patient with pen and paper. He found over time that the unrestricted use of these materials had a very calming effect on the patient. This finding led Dr Fischer to continue to explore the use of art not only with psychiatric patients, but with patients in his private practice as well as with children and adolescents in residential treatment. Dr Fischer also encouraged his psychiatric residents to employ art with their patients in the hope that this form of therapy would gain wider acceptance in the mental health profession. (1996a: 21)

In 1968 Dr Fischer founded the Toronto Art Therapy Institute in order to train art therapists and for over a decade this was the only available training in Canada. In 1977 Dr Fischer was also instrumental in founding the Canadian Art Therapy Association (CATA).

During the 1950s, the Dewdney's, both of whom had a background in art and a keen interest in psychoanalysis, began working at the Westminster Hospital in London, Ontario. In 1952 Selwyn Dewdney was appointed psychiatric art therapist, the first art therapy post to be established in Canada by the Federal Government. In 1954 his wife Irene joined him in his work. In 1972 Irene began working at the London Psychiatric Hospital in Ontario, as well as at several other psychiatric settings (Dewdney, 1991). As Irene Dewdney's work developed she became increasingly involved in training students, an interest that led to the formation of the art therapy programme at the University of Western Ontario in the early 1980s.

During the 1950s, the fourth major pioneer of art therapy in Canada, Marie Revai, also began her work in Montreal as an artist and teacher with a special interest in the needs of underprivileged children and adults. Later, in 1957, Revai was employed to work with psychiatric patients in the occupational therapy department of the Alan Memorial Hospital in Montreal. Marie Revai was to remain in Montreal for 19 years, during which time she nurtured a growing interest in art therapy in the Montreal community.

It was largely through the pioneering spirit of these early founders of the profession that art therapy in Canada first gained acceptance and later spread to other areas. British Columbia, for example, now supports three art therapy training programmes; the Kutenai Art Therapy Institute located in Nelson, the British Columbia School of Art Therapy in Victoria (Bradley, 1996) and the Vancouver Art Therapy Institute (Woolf, 1996b).

Art therapy in Canada has had to overcome considerable resistance and scepticism in order to establish itself sufficiently to compete with the medical establishment for public funding. However, in contrast to the situation in both the UK and USA, the profession lacks cohesion as it 'continues to attempt to resolve a long-standing split among art therapists which began with the profession's development' (Gilroy and Hanna, 1998: 253). Although this may, in part, be due to art therapy in Canada having, like the nation itself, developed along provincial lines, other factors have undoubtedly played a role. Of particular importance here has been the influence Dr Fischer exerted over the development of the profession until his death in 1992.

Dr Fischer and the Toronto Art Therapy Institute

The model of art therapy practice and training promoted by Dr Fischer at the Toronto Art Therapy Institute used images and objects in a manner similar to dreams in psychoanalysis, as the symbolic expression of unconscious thoughts and feelings (Fischer, 1973). The experiential methods of training Dr Fischer developed to support this model of art therapy were designed to help facilitate the spontaneous production of art. It was important, however, that the art therapist refrain from offering any interpretation of the art work since, in Fischer's view, 'this would contaminate the personal meaning each artwork has for its creator' (Gray, 1978: 492–493). The task of interpreting and attributing meaning to these artworks, be this for diagnostic or therapeutic purposes, was to be undertaken by Dr Fischer himself. In effect, art therapists were being trained to assume a subordinate role. As a consequence, 'Students felt inspired but ill-equipped to think critically about their roles as art therapists' (Stern, personal correspondence). Moreover, as Gilroy and Hanna comment,

> Student trainees at the Toronto Art Therapy Institute, with no art training, often worked side by side with highly skilled and gifted artists. This created an imbalance in the sensibility toward the art making process, and ambiguity regarding the identity of art therapists. Indeed, with students graduating from the programme with little formal art training, reinforcement was given to the position that anyone with training in psychology or psychiatry could also do art therapy. This significantly weakened the position of art therapists as unique professionals with a set of skills which set them apart from psychologists and other practicing psychotherapists and psychiatrists. In many ways this established a norm suggesting that art therapists were 'adjunct' therapists supporting the more firmly established and defined clinical skills of psychologists and psychiatrists. (1998: 254)

Thus, in addition to promoting his particular version of art therapy through his active involvement in the running of the Toronto Art Therapy Institute and, later, the Canadian Art Therapy Association, Dr Fischer was able to exert a controlling and conservative influence on the art therapy community in Canada (Gilroy and Hanna, 1998; Stern, 1997). Despite such criticisms, Fischer was a respected figure within the Canadian art therapy community and evidently did much to help promote art therapy across the country (Quinn, 1992; Seeley, 1992). Nevertheless, his authority and charisma also appear to have limited the extent to which Canadian art therapists have been able to establish an independent and self-directed identity for themselves. Such developments towards professional autonomy as have occurred within Canadian art therapy are largely due to increasing exposure to the influence of external developments in art therapy, especially those emanating from the USA, the establishing of alternative training courses offering different models of art therapy and the founding of provincial art therapy associations.

Art Therapy Training in Canada

Art therapy training in Canada, unlike that in the UK or USA, is based largely in private, post-secondary education institutions. The qualifications offered by these courses vary, but all are offered at post-baccalaureate level. There is also considerable variation in the nature and content of these training programmes (Woolf, 1996a). Despite these differences, art therapy training in Canada, as elsewhere in the world, consists of three main elements:

- Personal engagement with image making and psychotherapy aimed at enabling students to gain a personal understanding of the value of the art therapy process.
- Supervised practica (what, in the UK would be termed a clinical placement or fieldwork experience) through which students gain experience with a wide variety of client groups.
- Academic study.

Each element of this tripartite model of training is intended to help students develop both an experiential and theoretical appreciation of art therapy. In an attempt to maintain and improve standards the Canadian Art Therapy Association developed guidelines for the professional training of art therapists in 1995 (Simner, 1996a).

As noted above, it was largely due to the influence of Dr Fischer and, later, that of Selwyn and Irene Dewdney, that Ontario became the first centre for the training of art therapists in Canada. Indeed, following its founding in 1968, for many years the Toronto Art Therapy Institute provided the only art therapy training in Canada. The methods of training developed at the TATI were almost exclusively based on Dr Fischer's own beliefs and ideas (Fischer, 1973; Grossman, 1996). These emphasised the value of art as a mode of non-verbal, symbolic communication and as a means of externalising unconscious (repressed) thoughts, feelings and conflicts. The art therapy training developed at the Institute was primarily experiential, underpinned by Freudian theory. According to Grossman,

> From its inception the Institute has offered a concentrated approach to training with the goal of instructing therapists to become highly skilled and competent professionals able to work either as primary therapists or as an integral part of

> a multi-disciplinary team … As one means of achieving this goal, trainees must
> undergo in-depth self-exploration through personal psychotherapy. (1996: 33)

A background in art does not, however, appear to be regarded as a necessary prerequisite to becoming an art therapist, as is the case in both the UK
and the USA. Moreover, the methods of teaching employed, particularly in
the early life of the TATI, seemingly made little distinction between being
Fischer's client and being a trainee, or between being a teacher and being a
therapist. Nor were opportunities provided to critically examine alternative
approaches to the practice of art therapy (Stern, 1997). One consequence of
this blurring of boundaries was that Fischer became, for many Canadian art
therapists, a somewhat idealised figure. As Stern comments, for many of his
former students, 'Fischer *was* art therapy' (personal correspondence).

Over time, art therapy training in Canada extended beyond Toronto and
its surrounding area. In 1982, Lois Woolf, a graduate of the Toronto Art
Therapy Institute, established the Vancouver Art Therapy Institute (Woolf,
1996b) and in 1995, Monica Carpendale founded the Kutenai Art Therapy
Institute in Nelson, British Colombia. Both the Kutenai Art Therapy
Institute and the Vancouver Art Therapy Institute are modelled on Dr
Fischer's method of training art therapists. Importantly, in recognition of
the fact that art therapy in Canada has largely developed in the urban
conurbations, the Kutenai Art Therapy Institute was founded, as
Jacqueline Fehlner, the current President of the Canadian Art Therapy
Association comments, 'specifically to train art therapists to work in rural
communities and with First Nations People' (personal correspondence).

While Dr Fischer's influence on art therapy training in Canada has been
extensive, alternative models of training have emerged. In 1978 Michael
Edwards, an experienced art therapy educator from the UK, was invited
to develop art therapy training at Concordia University in Montreal. As a
result of the interest shown, Edwards returned to Concordia University
the following year and helped establish a diploma programme in art therapy under the auspices of the Art Education Department. In 1982 the programme began to offer art therapy training at masters level and in 1984
the official degree MA in Art Therapy was established (Peterson et al.,
1996). Significantly, the art therapy training offered at Concordia was
based in the Art Education Faculty of a university, 'thus refreshingly high-
lighting an emphasis on the significance of art skills in the training of art
therapists' (Gilroy and Hanna, 1998: 254). The Concordia University
course also has the distinction of being the only Canadian art therapy
training programme accredited by the American Art Therapy Association
and many of its graduates subsequently register with AATA rather than the
Canadian Art Therapy Association.

In 1983 the University of Western Ontario invited Linda Nicholas, a former student of Irene Dewdney, to run a course in art therapy. By 1987
enthusiasm for art therapy training in the London community had resulted
in the establishing of a two-year, post-baccalaureate, diploma programme
in art therapy (Simner, 1996b). In 1980, Kathleen Collis, a Canadian art

therapist who had strong connections with art therapists in the USA, founded an art therapy training programme at the Victoria Mental Health Centre in British Columbia. Initially run on an informal and part-time basis, by 1984 it had become a formal, full-time programme run under the auspices of the Victoria Institute of Art Therapy (later re-named the British Columbia School of Art Therapy) (Bradley, 1996).

Art therapy training programmes currently exist in three Canadian provinces and growing numbers of graduates are entering training on a yearly basis.

The Canadian Art Therapy Association

Unlike art therapy in the UK and USA, where the BAAT and AATA have been instrumental in promoting and developing the profession, in Canada the influence of the Canadian Art Therapy Association (CATA), formed in 1977, has not been as extensive. Founded, and first presided over by Dr Fischer, the CATA has suffered from some of the same difficulties as the Toronto Art Therapy Institute previously discussed. Stern comments,

> Conflicts of interest, a questionable claim to democratic functioning and factions have long characterised the Association. Underlying these issues is the question of representation: Who represents the professional body, and what is represented as the profession (personal correspondence).

Similar concerns regarding CATA's failure to effectively represent the professional interests of all art therapists in Canada are raised by Gilroy and Hanna who argue,

> This association, guided by a psychiatrist, greatly impacted on the direction of the profession in Canada as appointments to the Executive Committee of the Canadian Art Therapy Association were usually by invitation, and in this way input into the affairs of the association remained within a small group of followers committed to the training norms developed by a psychiatrist. (1998: 255)

Since 1994 the Canadian Art Therapy Association has had open elections, but remains dependent on the commitment of its members to undertake aspects of its work that larger organisations are able to pay for.

As a reaction to this perceived lack of democratic representation, and in order to both address local concerns and promote the discipline at a provincial level, significant numbers of Canadian art therapists channelled their energy into founding provincial art therapy associations. In 1978 the British Columbia Art Therapy Association was founded, and the following year witnessed the founding of the Ontario Art Therapy Association. Two years later, in 1981, the Quebec Art Therapy Association was formed. Although these provincial associations have thrived, and now exist wherever art therapy training is offered in Canada, this fragmentation of the profession has weakened the position of the Canadian Art Therapy Association in its attempts to promote the profession and improve standards of training nationally. As previously noted, another consequence has been that many Canadian art therapists have sought professional recognition by registering and seeking certification via the American Art Therapy Association and the Art Therapy Credentials Board.

Despite the foregoing difficulties, the Canadian Art Therapy Association continues to work towards resolving conflicts within the profession. Ongoing activities of the Association include the publication, since 1983, of a bi-annual journal, a newsletter and the convening of an annual conference.

Art Therapy in Australia

The history and development of art therapy in Australia is not well known outside its own borders. Moreover, what little is known about the profession in Australia may be found almost exclusively in accounts written by visiting European and North American art therapists (see, for example, Campanelli and Kaplan, 1996; Gilroy, 1998; Gilroy and Hanna, 1998). As Gilroy and Hanna comment,

> The work of the profession's founders prior to the inauguration of ANATA [the Australian National Art Therapy Association] is not yet fully documented but it is clear that artists, art teachers and occupational therapists were initiating their individual art therapy practice in much the same way as the profession began elsewhere in the world. (1998: 270)

The reasons why Australian art therapy is not better known are difficult to determine, but the fact that Australia is a huge and geographically remote continent and that the number of practicing art therapists is tiny undoubtedly play a part.

According to Henzell, an Australian national now leading the art therapy course at Edith Cowen University in Perth, Western Australia, after having worked and taught in the UK for many years, the practice of art therapy has explicit and implicit origins in its Australian setting. To be listed among the implicit artistic, cultural and social influences on art therapy are, Henzell suggests,

> Australia's 200 year history of colonisation and settlement, first of all by convicts and settlers from the British Isles with later influxes of migrants from European and many other countries, the resulting dispossession and persecution of its indigenous people, its participation in two world wars, the continent's vast and unique geography, and the distinctly Australian tradition of post-war painting epitomized by the work of Sydney Nolan, Albert Tucker, Arthur Boyd and Russell Drysdale. (Personal correspondence)

More overt influences on the development of art therapy in Australia have been the contributions made by the psychiatrists Ainslie Meares and Eric Cunningham Dax, the painter Guy Grey-Smith and pioneering work of art therapists themselves; many of whom trained in the UK or USA before returning or migrating to Australia.

The roles played by Meares and Cunningham Dax in the development of art therapy in Australia have been very different. Meares worked in Melbourne during the 1940s and 1950s, and is possibly best known to art therapists outside Australia through his book *The Door to Serenity* (Meares, 1958). This book provides a sympathetic account of Meares' work with a young woman – 'Jennifer' – for whom painting became a central feature of therapy; all other forms of treatment, including insulin coma and electro convulsive therapy, having failed. The influence exerted upon the development of art therapy by Dr E. Cunningham Dax on the other hand has, arguably, been less positive. Having been responsible for employing some of the first art therapists in the UK, including Edward Adamson (Adamson, 1990; Byrne, 1996; Hogan, 2000), Cunningham Dax went to Australia in 1952 to become Chairman of the newly formed Mental Health Authority, a post he held until 1969. In addition to establishing art studios similar to those in which Adamson was employed, and thereby extending his collection of 'psychiatric art' (Cunningham Dax, 1998), Cunningham Dax also appears to have been influential in promoting the view that art therapy be incorporated into occupational therapy, rather than allowed to develop as an autonomous, self-directed profession. A stance similar to that he had earlier adopted towards art therapy in the UK.

The painter Guy Grey-Smith's involvement with art therapy, by contrast, followed a very different path. During World War Two, Grey-Smith, who was serving in the Royal Air Force, had been shot down over Germany where he developed tuberculosis as a prisoner of war. While recuperating in Britain he met Adrian Hill who encouraged him to paint and draw 'for the relaxing and morale-boosting effects of artistic activity on seriously ill TB patients' (Henzell, 1997: 177). On his return to Australia after the war Grey-Smith began using Hill's version of art therapy with TB and psychiatric patients in Perth. He is now chiefly remembered in Australia as a prominent artist and campaigner for artists' rights. It was through meeting, and later working with Grey-Smith that Henzell, who later played an important role in establishing art therapy in the UK, first became involved with the profession (Henzell, 1997). Unfortunately, mainly due to the clinical conservatism of the psychiatric and clinical psychology professions, and the isolated nature of their work, pioneer art therapists such as Grey-Smith were unable to establish an independent profession. Henzell comments,

> Psychiatry and clinical psychology have exercised a controlling influence over treatment and therapy in the public sector and this has severely restricted the influence of psychotherapeutic and analytic ideas in this area; for example if someone is referred for psychotherapy the state will, generally speaking, only pay for therapy if an accredited psychiatrist or clinical psychologist conducts it. The result of this closed shop has been that for those who cannot afford to seek therapeutic help privately, therapy and counselling are largely of the cognitive and behavioural variety. (Personal correspondence)

The medical model of mental illness adhered to by the majority of Australian psychiatrists has not been modified by psychoanalytically based approaches to treatment found elsewhere in the world. As a consequence, art therapy has been less well received than in the UK and USA (Gilroy, 1998).

It was not until the 1980s, when overseas trained art therapists began to practice in Australia, that the growth of art therapy achieved any significant momentum. The energy of these pioneering art therapists was primarily directed towards securing employment, developing courses and organising and promoting the profession (Coulter-Smith, 1983; Gore, 1989). Steps that eventually led to the establishing of formal art therapy training courses and the formation of the Australian National Art Therapy Association in 1987. Despite the foregoing difficulties, art therapists in Australia may currently be found working in private practice, as well as in public and private agencies, prisons, family welfare agencies, nursing homes, rehabilitation centres, drug and alcohol units, women's health centres and community health centres.

Art Therapy Training in Australia

Australia currently hosts three postgraduate art therapy training courses dating from the late 1980s and the early to mid-1990s. Prior to this the only form of postgraduate study available was an MA in Creative Arts Therapies at La Trobe University in Melbourne, run by Warren Lett. However, although this course included art therapy, it was primarily dance and music therapy orientated. Since then, Australia has become one of the few countries outside Europe and North America to provide training in art therapy at postgraduate level and, as a consequence, increasing numbers of art therapists have completed trainings that meet agreed professional standards. In composition and duration, the three Australian MA art therapy training courses are very similar to the Postgraduate Diploma courses run in the UK (see Chapter 6).

The first of the Master's level art therapy training courses founded in Australia was at Edith Cowan University in Perth. A distinctive feature of the course at ECU is that it is based within an arts faculty (the School of Visual Arts within the Western Australian Academy of Performing Arts), whereas those at the University of Western Sydney and La Trobe University in Melbourne are run within health science faculties. Other differences between these courses may be detected regarding their philosophy, structure and theoretical orientation (Campanelli and Kaplan, 1996). However, as Campanelli and Kaplan (1996: 64) also note, 'these programmes are still in a formative stage and are likely to experience many changes in the next few years'. One such development has been that art therapy students increasingly undertake clinical placements in remote population centres working with refugees or clients from the indigenous population.

An important dynamic in this process of development is the extent to which these courses are able to integrate models of practice and training developed in the UK and USA with those best suited to the particular circumstances of Australian art therapy. This may, as Gilroy and Hanna (1998: 273) suggest, 'give rise to controversy, friction, tension and anxiety; but only through such a process will a uniquely Australian art therapy be formed'. The Australian art therapy training courses face two main difficulties in relation to this. These concern standards of entry into the profession and the employability of graduates. At the present time there are a number of courses running in Australia that claim to be training 'art therapists' but which do not meet the academic or professional standards established by the MA in Art Therapy courses run at Edith Cowan University, the University of Western Sydney and La Trobe University. Without recognised training standards such as those found in the UK and USA, the issue of who might legitimately lay claim to the title 'art therapist' is difficult to address. In an attempt to clarify matters, in 1992 the Australian National Art Therapy Association drafted its recommendations for art therapy training programmes at Master's degree level (ANATA, 1992). Unfortunately, because these recommendations were never fully complied with, ANATA, in collaboration with three existing MA courses, are currently in the process of rewriting the art therapy training guidelines through its Training and Accreditation Committee.

Because there is no equivalent to the Health Professions Council in Australia, a knock-on effect of this has been that graduates often experience difficulty in gaining employment within the existing health and community welfare systems after training. It would appear that those art therapists who graduate from the existing training courses are more likely to secure employment if, in addition to having a first degree in such fields as psychology, nursing, occupational therapy or education, they also have recognised qualifications in areas such as counselling, family therapy or child psychotherapy. It is to be hoped that as increasing numbers of qualified art therapists enter the workforce, and their training is more widely recognised, this situation will change.

The Australian National Art Therapy Association

The Australian National Art Therapy Association Inc. (ANATA) was founded in 1987, the first meeting being held in Brisbane, where the first National Conference was also held in 1989. At the founding meeting, most of the ten art therapists present were trained and registered in either the USA or the UK. ANATA offers support to practicing art therapists and others interested in the field by providing information on research and employment, in addition to promoting professional development through establishing standards for training, registration and clinical practice. Although the association does not yet have the resources to produce a journal, it does publish a newsletter four times a year. Among its current priorities, ANATA lists the following:

- Developing training opportunities and establishing criteria for the training of art therapists in Australia in accordance with international standards.
- Establishing a register of Art Therapists and to grant registration to those individuals who meets the required standards.
- Encouraging the development of Regional Groups. To date, groups of art therapists affiliated to ANATA have been established in South East Queensland, Victoria, Canberra and Perth.
- Supporting regulatory and legislative recognition.
- Offering conferences and courses to meet member's practice needs.
- Promoting the inclusion of art therapists as providers in managed care systems.
- Improving and maintaining working relationships with the US based Art Therapy Credentials Board.

Professional Membership of ANATA is by application and is open to all persons who have completed professional training in art therapy or its equivalent, as recognised by the Membership Committee.

ANATA is a Member Association of the Psychotherapy and Counselling Federation of Australia (PACFA), and art therapists who are Professional Members of ANATA can, after a further specified period of supervised practice, join the PACFA national register of accredited psychotherapists and counsellors in Australia and New Zealand. The connection between ANATA and PACFA is crucial to Australian art therapists. PACFA is gaining increasing government recognition, both federally and at State level, so challenging the closed shop operated by clinical psychologists. This monopoly made it virtually impossible for clients to receive Medicare funding or tax exemption if they sought psychotherapy in the public or private sector. The New South Wales State government recently ruled against this arrangement and it is anticipated that other States will introduce similar legislation in due course.

Notes

1. An edited collection of papers presented at past conferences has been published by Kossolapow et al. (2001).

2. The Menninger Clinic in Topeka, Kansas employed an art therapist, Mary Huntoon, as early as 1935. Regrettably, as many of these early art therapists worked in isolation and did not publish accounts of their practice, their contribution to the development of art therapy in the US remains largely unacknowledged.

3. In addition to teaching at the Walden School, Cane taught privately, lectured to teachers and in later life became the Director of Art for the Counselling Centre for Gifted Children at New York University; a position she held for 14 years. Regrettably, Florence Cane wrote only one book, *The Artist in Each of Us*, first published in 1951 (Cane, 1989).

APPENDIX 1: FURTHER READING

Art Therapy: An introductory reading list

Adamson, E. (1984) *Art as Healing*, London: Coventure Press.

Campbell, J., Liebmann, M., Brookes, F., Jones, J. and Ward, C. (eds) (1999) *Art Therapy, Race and Culture*, London: Jessica Kingsley.

Case, C. and Dalley, T. (1992) *The Handbook of Art Therapy*, London: Routledge.

Dalley, T., Case, C., Schaverien, J., Weir, F., Halliday, D., Nowell Hall, P. and Waller, D. (eds) (1984) *Art as Therapy*, London: Tavistock Publications.

Dalley, T. (1987) *Images of Art Therapy: New developments in theory and practice*, London: Tavistock Publications.

Dalley, T. and Case, C. (eds) (1992) *Working With Children in Art Therapy*, London: Routledge.

Dalley, T., Rifkind, G. and Terry, K. (1993) *Three Voices of Art Therapy: Image, Client, Therapist*, London: Routledge.

Gilroy, A. and Dalley, T. (eds) (1989) *Pictures At An Exhibition: Selected essays on art and art therapy*, London: Routledge.

Gilroy, A. and McNeilly, G. (eds) (2000) *The Changing Shape of Art Therapy*, London: Jessica Kingsley.

Hiscox, A.R. and Calisch, A.C. (eds) (1998) *Tapestry of Cultural Issues in Art Therapy*, London: Jessica Kingsley Publishers.

Hogan, S. (2001) *Healing Arts: The History of Art Therapy*, London: Jessica Kingsley.

Hogan, S. (ed.) (2002) *Gender Issues in Art Therapy*, London: Jessica Kingsley.

Hogan, S. (ed.) (1997) *Feminist Approaches to Art Therapy*, London: Routledge.

Junge, M. and Asawa, P. (1994) *A History of Art Therapy in The United States*, Mundelein, IL: The American Art Therapy Association, Inc.

Killick, K. and Schaverien, J. (eds) (1997) *Art, Psychotherapy and Psychosis*, London: Routledge.

Kramer, E. (2000) *Art as Therapy: Collected papers*, London: Jessica Kingsley.

Liebmann, M. (ed.) (1994) *Art Therapy with Offenders*, London: Jessica Kingsley.

Liebmann, M. (1999) *Art Therapy for Groups*, London: Routledge.

Liebmann, M. (ed.) (1990) *Art Therapy in Practice*, London: Jessica Kingsley.

Maclagan, D. (2001) *Psychological Aesthetics*, London: Jessica Kingsley.

Malchiodi, C.A. (ed.) (2002) *Handbook of Art Therapy*, New York: Guilford Press.

Murphy, J. (ed.) (2000) *Art Therapy with Young Survivors of Sexual Abuse*, London: Routledge.

Pratt, M. and Wood, M. (1998) *Art Therapy in Palliative Care*, London: Routledge.

Rees, M. (ed.) (1998) *Drawing on Difference: Art therapy with people with learning difficulties*, London: Routledge.

Rubin, J.A. (ed.) (2001) *Approaches to Art Therapy* (2nd edn), New York: Brunner-Routledge.

Rubin, J.A. (1999) *Art Therapy: An introduction*, Philadelphia: Brunner/Mazel.

Schaverien, J. (1991) *The Revealing Image*, London: Routledge.

Silverstone, L. (1997) *Art Therapy: The person-centred way* (2nd edn), London: Jessica Kingsley.

Simon, R.M. (1997) *Symbolic Images in Art as Therapy*, London: Routledge.

Simon, R.M. (1991) *The Symbolism of Style*, London: Routledge.

Skaife, S. and Huet, V. (eds) (1998) *Art Psychotherapy Groups*, London: Routledge.

Thomson, M. (1989) *On Art and Therapy*, London: Virago.

Wadeson, H. (2000) *Art Therapy Practice: Innovative Approaches with Diverse Populations*, New York: Wiley.

Waller, D. (1993) *Group Interactive Art Therapy: Its use in training and treatment*, London: Routledge.

Waller, D. and Gilroy, A. (eds) (1992) *Art Therapy: A handbook*, Milton Keynes: Open University Press.

APPENDIX 2: SOURCES OF FURTHER INFORMATION ON ART THERAPY

Professional associations

The British Association of Art Therapists
Suite 1089, Chancery Room
16-19 Southampton Place
London WC1A 2AJ
Tel: 020 7745 7262
E-mail: baat@ukgateway.net
Website: www.baat.org

American Art Therapy Association
E-mail: arttherapy@ntr.net
Website: www.arttherapy.org

Australian National Art Therapy Association
E-mail: secretary@anata.org.au
Website: www.anata.org.au/

Canadian Art Therapy Association
Website: http://home.ican.net/~phansen/pages/CATA.html

The British Columbia Art Therapy Association
Website: www.arttherapy.bc.ca/frames_main.html

The Ontario Art Therapy Association
Website: http://home.ican.net/%7Ephansen/pages/OATA.html

Association des art-thérapeutes du Québec
Website: http://iquebec.ifrance.com/aatq/english2.html

Addresses for other international art therapy associations can be found at
www.arttherapy.co.za/associations.htm

Art therapy journals

American Journal of Art Therapy
Website: www.norwich.edu/about/resources/pubs/ajat.html

Art Therapy: Journal of the American Art Therapy Association
Details available via the American Art Therapy Association website:
www.arttherapy.org

Inscape: Journal of the British Association of Art Therapists
Website: www.baat.org/inscape.html

The Arts in Psychotherapy
Website: www.elsevier.com/locate/issn/01974556

The Canadian Art Therapy Association Journal
Website: http://home.ican.net/~phansen/pages/ATjournal.html

UK art therapy training courses

Belfast
Graduate School of Education
Queen's University Belfast
69-71 University Street
Belfast BT7 1HL
Tel: 02890 335923
Website: www.qub.ac.uk

Derby
School of Health and Community Studies
University of Derby
Western Road
Mickleover
Derby DE3 5GX
Tel: 01332 592729
Website: www.derby.ac.uk

Edinburgh
School of Art Therapy
Queen Margaret College
Leith Campus
Duke Street
Edinburgh EH6 8HF
Tel: 0131 3173806
Website: www.qmced.ac.uk

Hatfield
Department of Art Therapies
Faculty of Art & Design
University of Hertfordshire
College Lane
Hatfield

Hertfordshire AL10 9AB
Website: www.herts.ac.uk

London
Art Psychotherapy
Unit of Psychotherapeutic Studies
Professional & Community Education
University of London
Goldsmiths College
23 St James
New Cross
London SE14 6AD
Tel: 020 79197230
Website: www.goldsmiths.ac.uk

Sheffield
The University of Sheffield
Art Psychotherapy
University Clinic
Leavygreave Road
Sheffield S5 7RE
Tel: 0114 2222964
Website: www.sheffield.ac.uk

Although these details are correct at the time of writing, within the next 12 to 18 months this training course will finish. It will be succeeded by the Northern Programme for Art Psychotherapy, a Sheffield-based joint venture between Sheffield Care Trust and Leeds Metropolitan University.

Information on art therapy training in Europe can be found at the
European Consortium for Arts Therapies Education (ECArTE) website:
www.uni-muenster.de/Ecarte/index.html

Further details regarding the educational programmes
currently approved by the American Art Therapy Association can be found at:
www.arttherapy.org/programmes.html

Further details regarding therapy training in Australia can be found at:
www.anata.org.au/attraining.htm

Further details regarding art therapy training in Canada can be found at:
http://home.ican.net/~phansen/pages/ATraining.html

Registration and careers information

The Health Professions Council
Park House
184 Kennington Park Road
London SE11 4BU
Tel: 020 7582 0866
E-mail: info@hpc-uk.org
Website: www.hpc-uk.org/

Listing of UK Registered Arts Therapists
Website: http://mipsweb.martex.uk.com/cpsm/regquerydb.asp?

The Art Therapy Credentials Board (ATCB)
E-mail: atcb@nbcc.org
Website: www.atcb.org/

NHS Careers information
Website: http://nhscareers.nhs.uk

Professional organisations

Art Therapists Practice Research Network
Email: atprn@gold.ac.uk
Website: www.baat.org/atprn.html

The International Society for the Psychopathology of Expression and Art Therapy (SIPE)
E-mail: sipearther@aol.com
Website: http://monsite.ifrance.com/art-therapy/art-therapy/000018124.htm

National Coalition of Arts Therapies Associations (NCATA)
Website: http://ncata.com

The National Network for the Arts in Health
Website: www.nnah.org.uk/main.htm

Northern Ireland Group for Art as Therapy (NIGAT)
Website: www.geocities.com/nigat_uk/index.html#1

The International Arts-Medicine Association
Website: http://members.aol.com/iamaorg/index.html

International Networking Group of Art Therapists (ING/AT)
E-mail: art_tx@earthlink.net

Irish Association of Creative Arts Therapists
Website: www.iacat.ie/about.html

Other useful addresses and websites

Adamson Collection
Website: www.slamart.org.uk/p2_artsprojects/adamson_collection.htm

Art Therapy in Canada
Website: www.arttherapyincanada.ca

Art Therapy in France
Website: http://arttherapie.com

Art Therapy on the Web
Website: www.sofer.com/art-therapy/index.html

Art Therapy Wiki
Website: www.sofer.com/cgi-bin/ArtTherapyWiki

Artworks in Mental Health
Website: www.artworksinmentalhealth.co.uk/index.asp

The Champernowne Trust: The Champernowne Trust does not currently have a website, but can be contacted c/o the Conference Secretary, Andrew Clements, 32 Meadfoot Lane, Torquay, Devon, TQ1 2BW.
E-mail: champernowne@aol.com

The Cunningham-Dax Collection
Website: http://members.ozemail.com.au/~ecdax/index.html

Freud Museum, London
Website: www.freud.org.uk/

Google: There are many useful search engines available to find information on the World Wide Web but one of the better ones is Google. Google also has the advantage of being able to conduct searches for images as well as text.
Website: www.google.com/

Government Mental Health Information
Website: www.doh.gov.uk/mentalhealth/index.htm

International Society For The Psychopathology of Expression and Art Therapy (SIPE)
Website: http://monsite.ifrance.com/art-therapy/art-therapy/000018124.htm

Jung Institute (Zurich)
Website: www.junginstitut.ch/index2.html

The Melanie Klein Trust
Website: www.melanie-klein-trust.org.uk/

National Electronic Library for Health
Website: www.nelh.nhs.uk/

Person-Centred Art Therapy
Website: www.person-centred-art-therapy.com/

POPAN
Website: www.popan.org.uk

The Prinzhorn Collection
Website: http://prinzhorn.uni-hd.de/im_ueberblick_eng.shtml

Raw Vision
Website: www.rawvision.com/

The Rita Simon Collection of Art Therapy
Website: www.wellcome.ac.uk/en/library/homlib/HOMlibCOLspeICOrsc.html

Scottish Arts Therapies Forum
Website: www.satf.org.uk

Squiggle Foundation
Website: www.squiggle-foundation.org.uk/

Theoretical Advances of Art Therapy (TAoAT)
Website: www.taoat.org/

Vicky Barber Homepage
Website: www.vickyb.demon.co.uk/

Virtual Arts Therapies Institute
Website: www.derby.ac.uk/research/vart/index.html

REFERENCES

Adams, L.S. (1993) *Art and Psychoanalysis*, New York: HarperCollins.

Adamson, E. (1990) *Art as Healing*, London: Coventure.

Agell, G. et al. (1981) Transference and countertransference in art therapy, *American Journal of Art Therapy*, 21(October): 3–24.

Alexander, F.G. and Selesnick, S.T. (1967) *The History of Psychiatry: An evaluation of psychiatric thought and practice from prehistoric times to the present*, London: Allen & Unwin.

Alexandrian, S. (1995) *Surrealist Art*, London: Thames and Hudson.

Alleyne, A. (1980) Finger painting: a projective technique, *Canadian Journal of Occupational Therapy*, 47(1): 23–26.

Alsop, A. (2000) *Continuing Professional Development: A guide for therapists*, Oxford: Blackwell Science.

Anastasi, A. and Foley, J.P. (1944) An experimental study of the drawing behaviour of adult psychotics in comparison with that of a normal control group, *Journal of Experimental Psychology*, 34: 169–194.

Atkinson, K. and Wells, C. (2000) *Creative Therapies: A psychodynamic approach within O.T.*, Cheltenham: Stanley Thornes.

(AATA) Australian National Art Therapy Association (1992) *Recommendations for Art Therapy Clinical Training Programmes at Masters Degree Level*, Glebe, New South Wales: ANATA.

Bannister, D. (1979) Foreword, in D. Rowe *The Experience of Depression*, Chichester: John Wiley & Sons.

Bateman, A. and Holmes, J. (1996) *Introduction to Psychoanalysis*, London: Routledge.

Bentley, T. (1989) Talking pictures, *Nursing Times*, 85(31, 2–8 August): 58–59.

Berger, J. (1965) *The Success and Failure of Picasso*, Harmondsworth: Penguin Books.

Berke, J. and Barnes, M. (1973) *Mary Barnes: Two accounts of a journey through madness*, Harmondsworth: Penguin Books.

Betensky, M.G. (1995) *What Do You See?* London: Jessica Kingsley.

Bion, W.R. (1967) *Second Thoughts*, London: Heinemann.

Birtchnell, J. (1986) Why don't British psychiatrists use art? *British Journal of Clinical and Social Psychiatry*, 4(1): 17–23.

Blain, G.H., Bergener, R.M., Lewis, M.L. and Goldstein, M.A. (1981) The use of objectively score able house-tree-person indicators to establish child abuse, *Journal of Clinical Psychology*, 37: 667–673.

Bowie, M. (1993) *Psychoanalysis and the Future of Theory*, Oxford: Blackwell.

Bradley, S. (1996) British Columbia School of Art Therapy Institute, *The Canadian Art Therapy Association Journal*, 10(1): 25–27.

Braithwaite, C. (1986) Art Always Reveals Truth, but Not Necessarily the Whole Truth, *Community Care*, July 31: 15–17.

(BAAT) British Association of Art Therapists (1978) Registration and training sub-committee report and recommendations, London: British Association of Art Therapists.

(BAAT) British Association of Art Therapists (1984) *Principles of Professional Practice for Art Therapists*, Brighton: British Association of Art Therapists.

(BAAT) British Association of Art Therapists (1992a) *Core Course Requirements for Postgraduate Art Therapy Training*, Brighton: British Association of Art Therapists.

(BAAT) British Association of Art Therapists (1992b) Art therapists and the law: sexual abuse (Occasional Paper), Brighton: British Association of Art Therapists.

(BAAT) British Association of Art Therapists (1994) *Code of Ethics and Principles of Professional Practice for Art Therapists*, Brighton: British Association of Art Therapists.

(BAAT) British Association of Art Therapists (2002) *State Registered Art Therapists Supervision Guidelines*, London: British Association of Art Therapists.

(BAAT) British Association of Art Therapists (2003) *Membership Directory 2003–2004*, London: British Association of Art Therapists.

Brock, M. (1991) The therapeutic use of clay, *Occupational Therapy*, 54: 13–15.

Buck, J.N. (1992) (Revised by Warren, W.L.) *House-Tree-Person Projective Drawing Technique Manual and Interpretive Guide*, Los Angeles, CA: Western Psychological Services.

Burns, R.C. and Kaufman, S.H. (1972) *Actions, Styles and Symbols in Kinetic Family Drawings (K-F-D): An interpretative manual*, New York: Brunner and Mazel.

Busine, L., Brand-Claussen, B., Douglas, C. and Jadi, I. (1998) *Beyond Reason: Art and psychosis, works from the Prinzhorn Collection*, San Francisco: University of California Press.

Byrne, P. (1980) Art therapy training and research at Birmingham Polytechnic-School of Art education, *Inscape* (Journal of the British Association of Art Therapists), 4(1): 4–7.

Byrne, P. (1987) Letter from LA, *Inscape* (Journal of the British Association of Art Therapists), Summer: 30–32.

Byrne, P. (1996) Edward Adamson and the experiment, *Inscape* (Journal of the British Association of Art Therapists), 1(1): 32–36.

Cagnoletta, M.D. (1990) Art therapy in Italy, *Inscape* (Journal of the British Association of Art Therapists), Summer: 23–25.

Cairns, F. (1994) A beginner's guide to transference and counter-transference within counselling, *Counselling*, November: 302–304.

Calish, A.C. (1998) Multicultural perspectives in art therapy supervision, in A.R. Hiscox and A.C. Calish (eds), *Tapestry of Cultural Issues in Art Therapy*, London: Jessica Kingsley Publishers.

Campanelli, M. and Kaplan, F.F. (1996) Art therapy in Oz: report from Australia, *The Arts in Psychotherapy*, 23(1): 61–67.

Campbell, J., Liebmann, M., Brookes, F., Jones, J. and Ward, C. (eds) (1999) *Art Therapy, Race and Culture*, London: Jessica Kingsley.

Cane, F. (1989) *The Artist in Each of Us*, Craftsbury Common, VT: Art Therapy Publications.

Cantle, T. (1983) Hate in the helping relationship: the therapeutic use of an occupational hazard, *Inscape* (Journal of the British Association of Art Therapists), October: 2–10.

Cardinal, R. (1972) *Outsider Art*, London: Studio Vista.

Carter, A. (1991) *The Virago Book of Fairy Tales*, London: Virago.

Case, C. (1990) The triangular relationship (3): the image as mediator, *Inscape* (Journal of the British Association of Art Therapists), Winter: 20–26.

Case, C. (1996) On the aesthetic moment in the transference, *Inscape* (Journal of the British Association of Art Therapists), 1(2): 39–45.

Case, C. (1998) Brief encounters: thinking about images in assessment, *Inscape* (Journal of the British Association of Art Therapists), 3(1): 26–33.

Case, C. (2000) 'Our lady of the queen': Journeys around the maternal object, in A. Gilroy and G. McNeilly (eds), *The Changing Shape of Art Therapy: New developments in theory and practice*, London: Jessica Kingsley.

Case, C and Dalley, T. (eds) (1990) *Working with Children in Art Therapy*, London: Routledge.

Case, C. and Dalley, T. (1992) *The Handbook of Art Therapy*, London: Routledge.

Casson, J. (2001) J.W. Von Goethe and J.C. Reil, *The British Journal of Psychodrama and Sociodrama*, 16(2): 118–127.

Cernuschi, C. (1992) *Jackson Pollock: 'Psychoanalytic' Drawings*, London: Duke University Press.

Champernowne, I. (1971) Art and therapy: an uneasy partnership, *Inscape* (Journal of the British Association of Art Therapists), 3: 2–14.

Charlton, S. (1984) Art therapy with long-stay residents of psychiatric hospitals, in T. Dalley (ed.), *Art as Therapy*, London: Tavistock Publications.

Chipp, H.B. (1973) *Theories of Modern Art*, Berkeley: University of California Press.

Clarke, L.M. and Willmuth, M.E. (1982) Art therapy: a learning experience for students in nursing, *Journal of Nursing Education*, 21(9 November): 24–27.

Cody, M. (2001) Going further with CPD, *BAAT Newsbriefing*, 10 March.

CORE System Group (1998) *CORE System (Information Management) Handbook*, Leeds: CORE System Group.

Coulter-Smith, A. (1983) Report from the Antipodes, *BAAT Newsletter*, December: 10–11.

CPSM Arts Therapists Board Disciplinary Committee (2000) *Statement of Conduct*, London: Committee for the Professions Supplementary to Medicine.

Culbertson, F.M. and Revel, A.C. (1987) Graphic characteristics on the draw-a-person test for identification of physical abuse, *Art Therapy*, 4(2): 78–83.

Cunningham Dax, E. (1953) *Experimental Studies in Psychiatric Art*, London: Faber and Faber.

Cunningham Dax, E. (1998) *The Cunningham Dax Collection: Selected Works of Psychiatric Art*, Melbourne: Melbourne University Press.

Dalley, T. (1984) *Art as Therapy*, London: Tavistock Publications.

Dalley, T. (2000) Thinking about theoretical developments in art therapy, in A. Gilroy and G. McNeilly (eds), *The Changing Shape of Art Therapy: New developments in theory and practice*, London: Jessica Kingsley.

Dalley, T., Rifkind, G. and Terry, K. (1993) *Three Voices of Art Therapy: Image, client, therapist*, London: Routledge.

Darnley-Smith, R. and Patey, H.M. (2003) *Music Therapy*, London: Sage.

Deco, S. (1998) Return to the open studio group, in S. Skaife and V. Huet (eds), *Art Psychotherapy Groups*, London: Routledge.

Department of Health (1999) *A National Service Framework for Mental Health*, London: Department of Health.

Department of Health (2001) *Clinical Guidelines for Treatment Choice Decision in Psychological Therapists and Counselling*, London: Department of Health.

Dewdney, I. (1991) The art therapist in the courtroom, *The Canadian Art Therapy Association Journal*, 6(1): 18–29.

Dollin, L. (1976) Art as a treatment medium in the psychiatric hospital, *Occupational Therapy*, September: 225–230.

Donnelly, M. (1984) Statement issued by the BAAT Council, concerning the Birmingham P.G.C.E. Art Therapy Option Course, at the BAAT EGM on 13 October 1984, *BAAT Newsletter*, December: 2–5.

Dube, W.-D. (1972) *The Expressionists*, London: Thames and Hudson.

Dudley, J., Gilroy, A. and Skaife, S. (1998) Learning from experience in introductory art therapy groups, in S. Skaife and V. Huet (eds), *Art Psychotherapy Groups*, London: Routledge.

Dudley, J. and Mahoney, J. (1991) In defence of 'Art psychotherapy', *BAAT Newsletter*, March: 11–12.

Duro, P. and Greenhalgh, M. (1993) *Essential Art History*, London: Bloomsbury.

Edwards, D. (1986) Three years on: surviving the institution, *Inscape* (Journal of the British Association of Art Therapists), Summer: 3–11.

Edwards, D. (1987) Evaluation in art therapy, in D. Milne (ed.), *Evaluating Mental Health Practice*, London: Croom Helm.

Edwards, D. (1989) Five years on: further thoughts on the issue of surviving as an art therapist, in A. Gilroy and T. Dalley (eds), *Pictures at an Exhibition*, London: Tavistock/Routledge.

Edwards, D. (1993a) Putting principles into practice, *Inscape* (Journal of the British Association of Art Therapists), Winter: 15–23.

Edwards, D. (1993b) Why don't arts therapists do research?, in H. Payne (ed.), *Handbook of Inquiry in the Arts Therapies: One River, Many Currents*, London: Jessica Kingsley.

Edwards, D. (1993c) Learning about feelings: the role of supervision in art therapy training, *The Arts in Psychotherapy*, 20: 213–222.

Edwards, D. (1994) On reflection: a note on supervision, *Inscape* (Journal of the British Association of Art Therapists), 1: 23–27.

Edwards, D. (1997) Endings, *Inscape* (Journal of the British Association of Art Therapists) 2(2): 49–56.

Edwards, D. (1999) The role of the case study in art therapy research, *Inscape* (Journal of the British Association of Art Therapists) 4(1): 2–9.

Edwards, D. (2002) On re-reading Marion Milner, *Inscape* (Journal of the British Association of Art Therapists) 6(1): 2–11.

Edwards, M. (1981) Art therapy now, *Inscape* (Journal of the British Association of Art Therapists), 5(1): 18–21.

Edwards, M. (1989) Art, therapy and Romanticism, in A. Gilroy and T. Dalley (eds), *Pictures at an Exhibition*, London: Tavistock/Routledge.

Ellenberger, H.F. (1994) *The Discovery of the Unconscious*, London: Fontana.

Elliott, D. (ed.) (1978) *The Inner Eye* (exhibition catalogue), Oxford: Museum of Modern Art.

Evans, J. (1979) Training in art therapy at Hertfordshire College of Art, *Inscape* (Journal of the British Association of Art Therapists) 3(2): 4–7.

Evans, K. and Dubowski, J. (2001) *Art Therapy with Children on the Autistic Spectrum*, London: Jessica Kingsley.

Feinberg, M. (1993) Training art therapy students to be supervisors: ethical and practical issues, *American Journal of Art Therapy*, 31(May): 109–112.

Fischer, M.A. (1973) Art as therapy, *Arts Magazine* (Society of Canadian Artists) 14(Spring-Summer): 7–8.

Fordham, F. (1973) *An Introduction to Jung's Psychology*, Harmondsworth: Penguin Books. This book is also available online at www.cgjungpage.org/fordhamintro.html

Freud, S. (1975) *The Standard Edition of the Complete Psychological Works of Sigmund Freud*. Translated and edited by James Strachey. London: Hogarth Press and the Institute of Psycho-Analysis.

Freud, S. (1979) *Introductory Lectures on Psychoanalysis*, The Pelican Freud Library, Volume 1, Harmondsworth: Penguin Books.

Freud, S. (1980) *The Interpretation of Dreams*, The Pelican Freud Library, Volume 4, Harmondsworth: Penguin Books.

Freud, S. (1991) *Group Psychology, Civilization and its Discontents and Other Works*, The Pelican Freud Library, Volume 12, Harmondsworth: Penguin Books.

Frye, B. (1990) Art and multiple personality disorder: an expressive framework for occupational therapy, *American Journal of Occupational Therapy*, 44(11): 1013–1022.

Fuller, P. (1980) *Art and Psychoanalysis*, London: Writers and Readers Press.

Fuller, P. (1983) Does therapy disrupt the creative process? *Inscape* (Journal of the British Association of Art Therapists), April: 5–7.

Gardner, W.H. (1985) *Gerard Manley Hopkins: Poems and prose*, Harmondsworth: Penguin Books.

Gilroy, A. (1989) On occasionally being able to paint, *Inscape* (Journal of the British Association of Art Therapists), Spring: 2–9.

Gilroy, A. (1992) Research in art therapy, in D. Waller and A. Gilroy (eds), *Art Therapy: A handbook*, Buckingham: Open University Press.

Gilroy, A. (1995) Change in art therapy groups, in A. Gilroy and C. Lee (eds), *Art and Music: Therapy and research*, London: Routledge.

Gilroy, A. (1996) Our own kind of evidence, *Inscape* (Journal of the British Association of Art Therapists), 1(2): 52–60.

Gilroy, A. (1998) On being a temporary migrant to Australia: reflections on art therapy education and practice, in D. Dokter (ed.), *Arts Therapists, Refugees and Migrants: Reaching across borders*, London: Jessica Kingsley.

Gilroy, A. (2001) Evidence based practice in art therapy, *BAAT Newsbriefing*, December: 2–3.

Gilroy, A. and Hanna, M. (1998) Conflict and culture in art therapy, in A.R. Hiscox and A.C. Calisch (eds), *Tapestry of Cultural Issues in Art Therapy*, London: Jessica Kingsley Publishers.

Gilroy, A. and Lee, C. (eds) (1995) *Art and Music: Therapy and Research*, London: Routledge.

Gilroy, A. and McNeilly, G. (eds) (2000) *The Changing Shape of Art Therapy*, London: Jessica Kingsley.

Gilroy, A. and Skaife, S. (1997) Taking the pulse of American art therapy, *Inscape* (Journal of the British Association of Art Therapists), 2(2): 57–64.

Glass, J. (1963) Art therapy, *Journal of the National Association for Mental Health*, 22(2).

Glover, N. (2000) Psychoanalytic aesthetics: the british school: available online at http://human-nature.com/free-associations/glover/index.html

Goffman, E. (1973) *Asylums*, Harmondsworth: Penguin Books.

Gomez, L. (1997) *An Introduction to Object Relations*, London: Free Association Books.

Goodenough, F. (1975) *Measures of Intelligence by Drawings*, New York: Arno Press.

Gordon, R. (1983) The creative process: self-expression and self-transcendence, in S. Jennings (ed.), *Creative Therapy*, Banbury: Kemble Press.

Gore, J. (1989) Conference review, *BAAT Newsletter*, December: 24–25.

Goss, S. and Rose, S. (2002) Evidence based practice: a guide for counsellors and psychotherapists, *Counselling and Psychotherapy Research*, 2(2): 147–151.

Gray, A. (1994) *An Introduction to the Therapeutic Frame*, London: Routledge.

Gray, C. (1978) Art therapy: when pictures speak louder than words, *Canadian Medical Association Journal*, 119(September 9): 488–532.

Greenberg, J.R. and Mitchell, S.A. (1983) *Object Relations in Psychoanalytic Theory*, London: Harvard University Press.

Greenwood, H. (1994) Cracked pots: art therapy and psychosis, *Inscape* (Journal of the British Association of Art Therapists), 1: 11–14.

Greenwood, H. and Layton, G. (1987) An out-patient art therapy group, *Inscape* (Journal of the British Association of Art Therapists), Summer: 12–19.

Grossman, G. (1996) Toronto art therapy institute, *Journal of the Canadian Art Therapy Association*, 10(1): 31–34.

Hacking, S. (1999) The psychopathology of everyday art: a quantitative study, unpublished PhD thesis, University of Keele. Available online at www.musictherapworld.de/modules/archive/stuff/papers/Hacking.pdf

Hacking, S. and Foreman, D. (2001) Psychopathology in paintings: a meta-analysis of studies using paintings by psychiatric patients, *British Journal of Medical Psychology*, 74: 35–45.

Hamer, N. (1993) Some connections between art therapy and psychodrama, *Inscape* (Journal of the British Association of Art Therapists), Winter: 23–26.

Hammer, E.F. (1958) *Clinical Application of Projective Drawing*, Springfield: Thomas.

Health Professions Council (2003) *Standards of Proficiency: Art therapists*, London: Health Professions Council. Available online at www.hpc-uk.org/publications/standards/Standards_of_Proficiency_Arts_Therapists.pdf

Henare, D., Hocking, C. and Smythe, L. (2003) Chronic pain: gaining understanding through the use of art, *British Journal of Occupational Therapy*, 66(11), 511–518.

Henzell, J. (1984) Art, psychotherapy, and symbol systems, in T. Dalley (ed.), *Art as Therapy*, London: Tavistock Publications.

Henzell, J. (1995) Research and the particular, in A. Gilroy and C. Lee (eds), *Art and Music: Therapy and research*, London: Routledge.

Henzell, J. (1997a) The images supervision, in G. Shipton (ed.), *Supervision of Psychotherapy and Counselling*, Buckingham: Open University Press.

Henzell, J. (1997b) Art, madness and anti-psychiatry: a memoir, in K. Killick and J. Schaverien (eds), *Art, Psychotherapy and Psychosis*, London: Routledge.

Herrmann U. (2000) Developing in splendid isolation? A critical analysis of German art therapy approaches in key papers from 1990 to 1999, *Inscape* (Journal of the British Association of Art Therapists) 5(1): 19–30.

Higgins, R. (1993) *Approaches to Case Study*, London: Jessica Kingsley.

Higgins, R. (1996) *Approaches to Research*, London: Jessica Kingsley.

Hill, A. (1948) *Art Versus Illness*, London: Allen and Unwin.

Hinshelwood, R.D. (1991) *A Dictionary of Kleinian Thought*, London: Free Association Books.

Hiscox, A.R. and Calisch, A.C. (eds) (1998) *Tapestry of Cultural Issues in Art Therapy*, London: Jessica Kingsley Publishers.

Hogan, S. (ed.) (1997) *Feminist Approaches to Art Therapy*, London: Routledge.

Hogan, S. (2000) British art therapy pioneer Edward Adamson: a non-interventionist approach, *History of Psychiatry*, XI: 250–271.

Hogan, S. (2001) *Healing Arts: The history of art therapy*, London: Jessica Kingsley.

Horgan, D. (1992) Bringing it all back home, *Inscape* (Journal of the British Association of Art Therapists), Winter: 2–5.

Horgan, D. (1998) Art therapy in Ireland, in D. Waller, *Towards a European Art Therapy: Creating a profession*, Buckingham: Open University Press.

Huet, V. (1997) Ageing, another tyranny: art therapy with older women, in S. Hogan (ed.), *Feminist Approaches to Art Therapy*, London: Routledge.

Hughes, R. (1981) *The Shock of the New*, London: British Broadcasting Corporation.

Huizinga, J. (1949) *Homo Ludens*, Translated by R.F.C. Hull, London: Routledge and Kegan Paul.

Jennings, S. and Minde, Å. (1995) *Art Therapy and Dramatherapy*, London: Jessica Kingsley.

Jones, E. (1916) The theory of symbolism, in papers on psychoanalysis (5th edn 1948), London: Hogarth Press.

Jones, G. (2000) An art therapy group in palliative cancer, *Nursing Times*, 96(10, 9–15 March): 42–43.

Jones, K. and Fowles, A.J. (1984) *Ideas on Institutions*, London: Routledge and Kegan Paul.

Jones, K., Stevens, P. and Richardson, P. (1998) A Randomised Trial of Group Based Art Therapy as an Adjunctive Treatment in Severe Mental Illness, unpublished paper delivered at The Third Theoretical Advances in Art Therapy Conference, Birmingham, 17 October.

Jung, C.G. (1969) *The Collected Works of C.G. Jung* (2nd edn). Translated by R.F.C. Hull, London: Routledge & Kegan Paul.

Jung, C.G. (ed.) (1978) *Man and his Symbols*, London: Picador.

Jung, C.G. (1985) *Memories, Dreams, Reflections*, London: Flamingo.

Jung, C.G. (1997) *Jung on Active Imagination*, London: Routledge.

Junge, M. and Asawa, P. (1994) *A History of Art Therapy in the United States*, Mundelein, IL: The American Art Therapy Association, Inc.

Kaye, C. and Blee, T. (eds) (1997) *The Arts in Health Care: A palette of possibilities*, London: Jessica Kingsley.

Kessler, M. (1993) Confidentiality, *American Journal of Art Therapy*, 31(May): 106–108.

Killick, K. (1991) The practice of art therapy with patients in acute psychotic states, *Inscape* (Journal of the British Association of Art Therapists), Winter: 2–6.

Killick, K. (1993) Working with psychotic processes in art therapy, *Psychoanalytic Psychotherapy*, 7(1): 25–38.

Killick, K. (2000) The art room as container in analytical art psychotherapy with patients in psychotic states, in A. Gilroy and G. McNeilly (eds), *The Changing Shape of Art Therapy*, London: Jessica Kingsley.

Killick, K. and Schaverien, J. (eds) (1997) *Art, Psychotherapy and Psychosis*, London: Routledge.

Klein, M. (1975) Narrative of a Child Analysis, in *The Writings of Melanie Klein*, Volume 4, London: The Hogarth Press and the Institute of Psycho-Analysis.

Knight, S. (1987) The use of art therapy for diabetics, *Practical Diabetes*, 4(5) September/October: 226–228.

Kossolapow, L., Scoble, S. and Waller, D. (2001) *Arts Therapies Communication: On the way to a communicative European arts therapy*, Volume 1, Münster: Lit-Verlag.

Kramer, E. (2000) *Art as Therapy: Collected papers*, London: Jessica Kingsley.

Kris, E. (1988) *Psychoanalytic Explorations in Art*, Madison, CT: International Universities Press.

Kwiatkowska, H.Y. (1978) *Family Art Therapy and Evaluation Through Art*, Springfield, IL: Charles C. Thomas Publishers.

Laing, J. (1984) Art therapy in prisons, in T. Dalley (ed.), *Art as Therapy*, London: Tavistock Publications.

Laing, R.D. (1970) *The Divided Self*, Harmondsworth: Penguin Books.

Laing, R.D. (1975) *Self and Others*, Harmondsworth: Penguin Books.

Lakoff, G. and Johnson, M. (1980) *Metaphors we Live By*, Chicago, IL: University of Chicago Press.

Landgarten, H. (1981) *Clinical Art Therapy: A comprehensive guide*, New York: Brunner/Mazel.

Lanham, R. (2002) Inscape revisited, *Inscape* (Journal of the British Association of Art Therapists), 7(2): 48–59.

Laplanche, J. and Pontalis, J.B. (1988) *The Language of Psycho-Analysis*. Translated by Donald Nicholson-Smith. London: Karnac & The Institute of Psycho-Analysis.

Lett, W.R. (1995) Experiential supervision through drawing and talking, *The Arts in Psychotherapy*, 22(4): 315–328.

Levens, M. (1995) *Eating Disorders and Magical Control of the Body: Treatment through art therapy*, London: Routledge.

Liebmann, M. (1981) The many purposes of art therapy, *Inscape* (Journal of the British Association of Art Therapists), 5(1): 26–28.

Liebmann, M. (1999) *Art Therapy for Groups*, London: Routledge.

Lloyd, C. and Papas, V. (1999) Art as therapy within occupational therapy in mental health settings: a review of the literature, *British Journal of Occupational Therapy*, 62(1): 31–35.

Lomas, P. (1994) *Cultivating Intuition*, London: Penguin Books.

Lyddiatt, E.M. (1971) *Spontaneous Painting and Modelling: A practical approach in therapy*, London: Constable.

MacGregor, J.M. (1989) *The Discovery of the Art of the Insane*, Princeton, NJ: Princeton University Press.

Machover, K. (1949) *Personality Projection in the Drawing of the Human Figure*, Springfield, IL: Charles C. Thomas Publishers.

Maclagan, D. (1983) Freud and the figurative, *Inscape* (Journal of the British Association of Art Therapists), October: 10–12.

Maclagan, D. (1984) Book review: art as healing by Edward Adamson, *Inscape* (Journal of the British Association of Art Therapists) Winter: 15.

Maclagan, D. (1993) A keen eye: outsider art and art therapy; aesthetics, ethics and cruelty, *Inscape* (Journal of the British Association of Art Therapists), Winter: 9–14.

Maclagan, D. (1997) Fantasy, play and the image in supervision, in G. Shipton (ed.), *Supervision of Psychotherapy and Counselling*, Buckingham: Open University Press.

Maclagan, D. (1999) Getting the feel: problems of research in fields of psychological aesthetics and art therapy, *The Arts in Psychotherapy*, 26(5): 303–311.

Maclagan, D. (2001) *Psychological Aesthetics*, London: Jessica Kingsley.

Maizels, J. (1996) *Raw Creation: Outsider art and beyond*, London: Phaidon.

Malchiodi, C.A. (1990) *Breaking the Silence*, New York: Brunner/Mazel.

Malchiodi, C.A. (ed.) (1999a) *Medical Art Therapy with Adults*, London: Jessica Kingsley.

Malchiodi, C.A. (ed.) (1999b) *Medical Art Therapy with Children*, London: Jessica Kingsley.

Malchiodi, C.A. (ed.) (2002) *Handbook of Art Therapy*, New York: Guilford Press.

Males, J. (1980) Art therapy: investigations and implications, *Inscape* (Journal of the British Association of Art Therapists), 4(2): 13–15.

Mann, D. (1988) Countertransference: a case of inadvertent holding, *Inscape* (Journal of the British Association of Art Therapists), Summer: 9–13.

Mann, D. (1989) The talisman or projective identification? A critique, *Inscape* (Journal of the British Association of Art Therapists), Autumn: 11–15.

Mann, D. (1990a) Art as a defence mechanism against creativity, *British Journal of Psychotherapy*, 7(1): 5–14.

Mann, D. (1990b) Some further thoughts on projective identification in art therapy, *Inscape* (Journal of the British Association of Art Therapists), Winter: 33–35.

Mann, D. (1991) Some schizoid processes in art psychotherapy, *Inscape* (Journal of the British Association of Art Therapists), Summer: 12–17.

Manning, T.M. (1987) Aggression depicted in abused children's drawings, *The Arts in Psychotherapy*, 14: 15–24.

Mayo, S. (1996) Symbol, metaphor and story: the function of group art therapy in palliative care, *Palliative Medicine*; 10(3) July: 209–16.

McLeod, J. (1995) *Doing Counselling Research*, London: Sage.

McLeod, J. (1997) *Narrative and Psychotherapy*, London: Sage.

McMurray, M. and Schwartz, M.O. (1998) Transference in art therapy: a new outlook, *The Arts in Psychotherapy*, 25(1): 31–36.

McNeilly, G. (1983) Directive and non-directive approaches in art therapy, *The Arts in Psychotherapy*, 10: 211–219.

McNeilly, G. (1984) Group-analytic art therapy, *Group Analysis*, XVII(3): 204–210.

McNeily, G. (1987) Further contributions to group analytic art therapy, *Inscape* (Journal of the British Association of Art Therapists), Summer: 8–11.

McNiff, S.A. (1979) From Shamanism to art therapy, *Art Psychotherapy*, 6: 155–161.

McNiff, S.A. (1987) Research and scholarship in the creative arts therapies, *The Arts in Psychotherapy*, 14: 285–292.

McNiff, S.A. (2000) *Art-Based Research*, London: Jessica Kingsley Publishers.

Meares, A. (1958) *The Door to Serenity*, London: Faber and Faber.

Meekums, B. (2002) *Dance Movement Therapy*, London: Sage.

Mental Health Foundation (1999) *The Fundamental Facts*, London: Pavillion.

Menzies, I. (1977) *The Functioning of a Social System as a Defence Against Anxiety*, London: Tavistock Publications.

Miller, A. (1996) *Pictures of a Childhood*, New York: Penguin USA.

Milner, M. (1952) Aspects of symbolism and comprehension of the not-self, *International Journal of Psychoanalysis*, 33: 181–195.

Milner, M. (1971) *On Not Being Able to Paint*, London: Heinemann.

Milner, M. (1988) *The Hands of the Living God*, London: Virago.

Milner, M. (1996) *The Suppressed Madness of Sane Men*, London: Routledge.

Mitchell, J. (ed.) (1986) *The Selected Melanie Klein*, Harmondsworth: Penguin Books.

Mollon, P. (1989) Anxiety, supervision and a space for thinking: some narcissistic perils for clinical psychologists in learning psychotherapy, *British Journal of Medical Psychology*, 62: 113–122.

Mollon, P. (2000) *The Unconscious*, Cambridge: Icon Books.

Molloy, T. (1997) Art psychotherapy and psychiatric rehabilitation, in K. Killick and J. Schaverien (eds), *Art, Psychotherapy and Psychosis*, London: Routledge.

Monroe, C.J. and Herron, S. (1980) Projective art used as an integral part of an intensive group therapy experience, *Occupational Therapy*, January: 21–24.

Moon, B. (2000) *Ethical Issues in Art Therapy*, Springfield, IL: Charles C. Thomas Publishers.

Moon, C.H. (2001) *Studio Art Therapy: Cultivating the artist identity in the art therapist*, London: Jessica Kingsley.

Moustakas, C. (1990) *Heuristic Research: Design, methodology and application*, London: Sage.

Murdin, L. (2000) *How Much is Enough?* London: Routledge.

Naumberg, M. (1947) *Studies of the Free Expression of Behaviour Disturbed Children as a Means of Diagnosis and Therapy*, New York: Grune and Stratton.

Naumberg, M. (1950) *Schizophrenic Art: Its meaning in psychotherapy*, New York: Grune and Stratton.

Naumberg, M. (1966) *Dynamically Oriented Art Therapy: Its principles and practice*, New York: Grune and Stratton.

Neale, E. and Rosal, M. (1993) What can art therapists learn from the research on projective drawing techniques for children? A review of the literature, *The Arts in Psychotherapy*, 20: 37–40.

Office of National Statistics (2000) *Psychiatric Morbidity Among Adults Living in Private Households in Great Britain*, ONS: London. Available at www.statistics.gov. uk/default.asp

Parry, G. (1997) Bambi fights back: psychotherapy research and service improvement, *Inscape* (Journal of the British Association of Art Therapists), 2(1): 11–13.

Paterson, C.F. (2002) A short history of occupational therapy, in J. Creek (ed.), *Occupational Therapy and Mental Health*, Edinburgh: Churchill Livingstone.

Patrick, J. and Winship, G. (1994) Creative therapy and the question of disposal: what happens to created pieces following the session? *British Journal of Occupational Therapy*, 57(1): 20–22.

Payne, H. (ed.) (1993) *Handbook of Inquiry in the Arts Therapies: One river, many currents*, London: Jessica Kingsley.

Peterson, L., Byers, J. and Gregoire, P. (1996) Concordia University, *Journal of the Canadian Art Therapy Association*, 10(1): 28–30.

Petocz, A. (1999) *Freud, Psychoanalysis and Symbolism*, Cambridge: Cambridge University Press.

Phillips, A. (1988) *Winnicott*, London: Fontana Press.

Pickford, R.W. (1967) *Studies in Psychiatric Art*, Springfield, IL: Charles C. Thomas Publishers.

Porter, R. (2002) *Madness: A brief history*, Oxford: Oxford University Press.

Pratt, M. and Wood, M. (1998) *Art Therapy in Palliative Care*, London: Routledge.

Prinzhorn, H. (1995) *Artistry of the Mentally Ill*. Translated by Eric von Brockdorff. New York: Springer-Verlag.

Quinn, T. (1992) Dr Martin Fischer: Canadian pioneer, *BAAT Newsletter*, June: 19–20.

Rawcliffe, T. (1987) A few of my own experiences of painting in relation to Marion Milner's Book, 'On Not Being Able to Paint', *Inscape*, Summer: 20–22.

Rees, M. (ed.) (1998) *Drawing on Difference: Art therapy with people with learning difficulties*, London: Routledge.

Reitman, F. (1950) *Psychotic Art*, London: Routledge & Kegan Paul.

Reynolds M.W., Nabors, L. and Quinlan, A. (2000) The effectiveness of art therapy: Does it work? *Art Therapy: Journal of the American Art Therapy Association*, 17(3): 207–213.

Rhodes, C. (1994) *Primitivism and Modern Art*, London: Thames and Hudson.

Rhodes, C. (2000) *Outsider Art*, London: Thames and Hudson.

Richardson, S. (2001) Who do they think we are? *BAAT Newsletter*, December: 6–9.

Robbins, A. (1994) *A Multi-Modal Approach to Creative Art Therapy*, London: Jessica Kingsley.

Roberts, J.P. (1984) Resonance in art groups, *Group Analysis*, XVII(3): 211–220.

Robinson, N. (1992) Art therapy in Switzerland, *Inscape* (Journal of the British Association of Art Therapists) Winter: 5–8.

Roth, P. (2001) *The Superego*, Cambridge: Icon Books.

Rowe, D. (1978) *The Experience of Depression*, Chichester: John Wiley & Sons.

Rowe, D. (1984) *Depression: The way out of your prison*, London: Routledge & Kegan Paul.

Rubin, J.A. (1999) *Art Therapy: An introduction*, Philadelphia, PA: Brunner/Mazel.

Rubin, J.A. (ed.) (2001) *Approaches to Art Therapy* (2nd edn), New York: Brunner-Routledge.

Rust, M.-J. (1987) Images and Eating Problems, in M. Lawrence (ed.), *Fed Up and Hungry*, London: The Women's Press.

Rust, M.-J. (1992) Art therapy in the treatment of women with eating disorders, in D. Waller and A. Gilroy (eds), *Art Therapy: A handbook*, Buckingham: Open University Press.

Rycroft, C. (1979) *A Critical Dictionary of Psychoanalysis*, Harmondsworth: Penguin.

Rycroft, C. (1981) *The Innocence of Dreams*, Oxford: Oxford University Press.

Salzberger-Wittenberg, I. (1991) *Psycho-Analytic Insight and Relationships*, London: Routledge.

Salzberger-Wittenberg, I., Henry, G. and Osborne, E. (1992) *The Emotional Experience of Learning and Teaching*, London: Routledge.

Samuels, A., Shorter, B. and Plaut, F. (1986) *A Critical Dictionary of Jungian Analysis*, London: Routledge & Kegan Paul.

Sayers, J. (2000) *Kleinians: Psychoanalysis inside out*, Cambridge: Polity Press.

Schaverien, J. (1982) Transference as an aspect of art therapy, *Inscape* (Journal of the British Association of Art Therapists), September: 10–16.

Schaverien, J. (1987) The scapegoat and the talisman: transference in art therapy, in T. Dalley, C. Case, J. Schaverien, F. Weir, D. Halliday, P. Nowell Hall and D. Waller (eds), *Images of Art Therapy*, London: Routledge.

Schaverien, J. (1989) Transference and the picture: art therapy in the treatment of anorexia, *Inscape* (Journal of the British Association of Art Therapists), Spring: 14–17.

Schaverien, J. (1990) The triangular relationship (2): desire, alchemy and the picture, *Inscape* (Journal of the British Association of Art Therapists), Winter: 14–19.

Schaverien, J. (1992) *The Revealing Image*, London: Routledge.

Schaverien, J. (1994) Analytical art psychotherapy: further reflections on theory and practice, *Inscape* (Journal of the British Association of Art Therapists), 2: 41–49.

Schaverien, J. (1995) *Desire and the Female Therapist*, London: Routledge.

Schaverien, J. (2000) The triangular relationship and the aesthetic countertransference in analytical art psychotherapy, in A. Gilroy and G. McNeilly (eds), *The Changing Shape of Art Therapy*, London: Jessica Kingsley.

Scull, A. (ed.) (1981) *Madhouses, Mad-Doctors and Madmen: The social history of psychiatry in the Victorian era*, Philadelphia: University of Pennsylvania Press.

Scull, A. (1993) *The Most Solitary of Afflictions: Madness and society in Britain 1700–1900*, New Haven, CT and London: Yale University Press.

Seeley, J.R. (1992) At the funeral of Dr Martin Aaron Fischer, *The Canadian Art Therapy Association Journal*, 6(2): 1–3.

Segal, A. (1942) *Art and Psychotherapy*, London: Guild of Pastoral Psychology.

Segal, H. (1978) *Introduction to the Work of Melanie Klein* (2nd edn), London: The Hogarth Press and The Institute of Psycho-Analysis.

Segal, H. (1991) *Dream, Phantasy and Art*, London: Routledge.

Segal, J. (1985) *Phantasy in Everyday Life*, Harmondsworth: Penguin Books.

Segal, J. (1992) *Melanie Klein*, London: Sage.

Segal, J. (2000) *Phantasy*, Cambridge: Icon Books.

Selz, P. (1974) *German Expressionist Painting*, Berkeley, Los Angeles: University of California Press.

Senior, P. and Croall, J. (1993) *Helping to Heal: The arts in health care*, London: The Calouste Gulbenkian Foundation.

Shorther, E. (1997) *A History of Psychiatry: From the era of asylum to the age of prozac*, New York: John Wiley.

Silverstone, L. (1997) *Art Therapy: The person-centred way* (2nd edn), London: Jessica Kingsley.

Simner, M.L. (1996a) University of Western Ontario, *The Canadian Art Therapy Association Journal*, 10(1): 35–37.

Simner, M.L. (1996b) Guidelines for the professional training of art therapists in Canada, *Canadian Art Therapy Association Journal*, 10(1): 40–42.

Simon, R. (1988) Marion Milner and the psychotherapy of art, *Winnicott Studies*, 3: 48–52.

Simon, R. (1992) *The Symbolism of Style*, Routledge: London.

Simon, R. (1997) *Symbolic Images in Art as Therapy*, Routledge: London.

Skaife, S. (1990) Self-determination in group analytic art therapy, *Group Analysis*, 23: 237–244.

Skaife, S. (1993) Sickness, health and the therapeutic relationship, *Inscape* (Journal of the British Association of Art Therapists), Summer: 24–29.

Skaife, S. (1995) The dialectics of art therapy, *Inscape* (Journal of the British Association of Art Therapists), 1: 2–7.

Skaife, S. (2000) Keeping the balance: further thoughts on the dialectics of art therapy, in A. Gilroy and G. McNeilly (eds), *The Changing Shape of Art Therapy*, London: Jessica Kingsley.

Skaife, S. (2001) Making visible: art therapy and intersubjectivity, *Inscape* (Journal of the British Association of Art Therapists), 6(2): 40–50.

Skaife, S. and Huet, V. (eds) (1998) *Art Psychotherapy Groups*, London: Routledge.

Skailes, C. (1997) The forgotten people, in K. Killick and J. Schaverien (eds), *Art, Psychotherapy and Psychosis*, London: Routledge.

Stern, E.-M. (1997) Some beginnings of art therapy in Canada; or the aesthetics of dependency, unpublished MA in Art Therapy dissertation, London: Goldsmiths College.

Stern, R. and Honore, E. (1969) The problem of national organisation: make haste slowly, *Bulletin of Art Therapy*, 8(3): 91–95.

Stevens, A. (1986) *The Withymead Centre: A Jungian community for the healing arts*, London: Coventure.

Stitelmann, J. (1998) Art therapy in Switzerland, in D. Waller (ed.), *Towards a European Art Therapy: Creating a profession*, Buckingham: Open University Press.

Storr, A. (1972) *The Dynamics of Creation*, London: Secker and Warburg.

Storr, A. (1990) *Solitude*, London: Fontana Paperbacks

Strand, S. (1990) Counteracting isolation: group art therapy for people with learning difficulties, *Group Analysis*, 23: 255–263.

Swan-Foster, N., Lawlor, M., Scott, L., Angel, D., Ruiz, C.M. and Mana, M. (2001) Inside an art therapy group: the student perspective, *The Arts in Psychotherapy*, 28: 161–174.

Szasz, T.S. (1974) *Ideology and Insanity*, Harmondsworth: Penguin Books.

Szasz, T.S. (1977) *The Myth of Mental Illness*, St Albans: Paladin.

Thomas, G.V. and Jolly, R.P. (1998) Drawing conclusions: a re-examination of empirical and conceptual bases for psychological evaluation of children from their drawings, *British Journal of Clinical Psychology*, 37(2, May): 27–39.

Thomson, M. (1992) Liminality and structure: art therapy-art psychotherapy, *BAAT Newsletter*, March: 20–21.

Thomson, M. (1997) *On Art and Therapy*, London: Virago.

Tipple, R. (1992) Art therapy with people who have severe learning difficulties, in D. Waller and A. Gilroy (eds), *Art Therapy: A handbook*, Buckingham: Open University Press.

Tipple, R. (1993) Challenging assumptions: the importance of transference processes in work with people with learning difficulties, *Inscape* (Journal of the British Association of Art Therapists), Summer: 2–9.

Tipple, R. (1994) Communication and interpretation in art therapy with people who have a learning disability, *Inscape* (Journal of the British Association of Art Therapists), 2: 31–35.

Tipple, R. (1995) The 'primitive' in art therapy, *Inscape* (Journal of the British Association of Art Therapists), 2: 10–18.

Trowbridge, M.M. (1995) Graphic indicator of sexual abuse in children's drawings: a review of the literature, *The Arts in Psychotherapy*, 22(5): 485–493.

Ulman, E. (2001) Art therapy: Problems of definition, *American Journal of Art Therapy*, 40(August): 16–26.

Vasarhelyi, V. (1992) Visual psychotherapy: the Hungarian challenge, *Inscape* (Journal of the British Association of Art Therapists), Winter: 21–33.

Vaughan, W. (1995) *Romanticism and Art*, London: Thames and Hudson.

Wadeson, H. (ed.) (1992) *A Guide To Conducting Art Therapy Research*, Mundelein, IL: The American Art Therapy Association.

Wadeson, H. (1994) *The Dynamics of Art Psychotherapy*, New York: Wiley.

Wadeson, H. (2000) *Art Therapy Practice: Innovative approaches with diverse populations*, New York: Wiley.

Waller, D. (1979) Art therapy training at University of London Goldsmiths College: Personal Reflections, *Inscape* (Journal of the British Association of Art Therapists), 3(2): 9–11.

Waller, D. (1987) Art therapy in adolescence, in T. Dalley, C. Case, J. Schaverien, F. Weir, D. Halliday, P. Nowell Hall and D. Waller (eds), *Images of Art Therapy: New developments in theory and practice*, London: Tavistock Publications.

Waller, D. (1989) Creative therapies, *BAAT Newsletter*, June: 25–26.

Waller, D. (1991) *Becoming a Profession: A history of art therapists 1940–82*, London: Routledge.

Waller, D. (1992a) The training of art therapists: past, present and future issues, in D. Waller and A. Gilroy (eds), *Art Therapy: A handbook*, Buckingham: Open University Press.

Waller, D. (1992b) The development of art therapy in Italy: some problems of definition and context in training and professional practice, *Inscape* (Journal of the British Association of Art Therapists) Winter: 8–17.

Waller, D. (1993) *Group Interactive Art Therapy: Its use in training and treatment*, London: Routledge.

Waller, D. (1998) *Towards a European art therapy: Creating a profession*, Buckingham: Open University Press.

Waller, D. (1999) The arts therapists open their register, *British Journal of Therapy and Rehabilitation*, 6(3) March: 110–111.

Waller, D. (ed.) (2002) *Arts Therapies and Progressive Illness: Nameless dread*, London: Brunner-Routledge

Waller, D. and Gilroy, A. (eds) (1978) *Ideas in Art Therapy*, London: British Association of Art Therapists.

Waller, D. and Mahoney, J. (eds) (1998) *Treatment of Addiction: Current issues for art therapists*, London: Routledge.

Watkins, M.M. (1981) Six approaches to the image in art therapy, *Spring* (An Annual of Archetypal Psychology and Jungian Thought), 107–125.

Weir, F. (1987) The role of symbolic expression in its relation to art therapy: a Kleinian approach, in T. Dalley, C. Case, J. Schaverien, F. Weir, D. Halliday, P. Nowell Hall and D. Waller (eds), *Images of Art Therapy: New developments in theory and practice*, London: Tavistock Publications.

Wilkins, P. (1999) *Psychodrama*, London: Sage.

Wilson, L., Riley, S. and Wadeson, H. (1984) Art therapy supervision, *Art Therapy: Journal of the American Art Therapy Association*, 1(3) October: 100–105.

Winnicott, D.W. (1971) *Therapeutic Consultations in Child Psychiatry*, London: The Hogarth Press and the Institute of Psycho-Analysis.

Winnicott, D.W. (1980) *Playing and Reality*, Harmondsworth: Penguin Books.

Woddis, J. (1984) The 14th Annual American Art Therapy Association Conference, *Inscape* (Journal of the British Association of Art Therapists), Summer: 11–13.

Woddis, J. (1986) Judging by appearances, *The Arts in Psychotherapy*, 13: 147–149.

Woddis, J. (1992) Art therapy: new problems, new solutions? in D. Waller and A. Gilroy (eds), *Art Therapy: A handbook*, Buckingham: Open University Press.

Wolff, H.H. (1977) Loss: a central theme in psychotherapy, *British Journal of Psychotherapy*, 13(3): 11–19.

Wolpert, L. (1999) *Malignant Sadness*, London: Faber and Faber.

Wood, C. (1986) Milk white panic, *Inscape* (Journal of the British Association of Art Therapists), Winter: 2–7.

Wood, C. (1990) The triangular relationship (1): The beginnings and endings of art therapy relationships, *Inscape* (Journal of the British Association of Art Therapists), Winter: 7–13.

Wood, C. (1991) A personal view of Laing and his influence on art therapy, *Inscape* (Journal of the British Association of Art Therapists), Winter: 15–18.

Wood, C. (1992) Using art therapy with 'chronic' long-term psychiatric patients, in D. Waller and A. Gilroy (eds), *Art Therapy: A handbook*, Buckingham: Open University Press.

Wood, C. (1997) The history of art therapy and psychosis (1938–1995), in K. Killick and J. Schaverien (eds), *Art, Psychotherapy and Psychosis*, London: Routledge.

Wood, C. (1999) Gathering evidence: Expansion of art therapy research strategy, *Inscape* (Journal of the British Association of Art Therapists), 4(2): 51–61.

Wood, C. (2000) The significance of studios, *Inscape* (Journal of the British Association of Art Therapists), 5(2): 40–53.

Wood, M. (1996) Art therapy and eating disorders: Theory and practice in Britain, *Inscape* (Journal of the British Association of Art Therapists), 1(1): 13–19.

Woodmansey, A.C. (1989) Internal conflict, *British Journal of Psychotherapy*, 6(1): 26–49.

Woolf, L. (1996a) History of art therapy training in Canada, *The Canadian Art Therapy Association Journal*, 10(1): 21–24.

Woolf, L. (1996b) Vancouver Art Therapy Institute, *The Canadian Art Therapy Association Journal*, 10(1): 38–39.

Yallom, I.D. (1970) *The Theory and Practice of Group Psychotherapy*, New York: Basic Books.

Young, R.M. (1998) The analytic frame, abstinence and acting out. Available online at http://human-nature.com/rmyoung/papers/pap11oh.htm

INDEX